IN HIS SERVICE

—— BOOK 3 ——

FAITH IN ACTION

IN HIS SERVICE

—— BOOK 3 ——

The Stories of Martin Luther King,
Father Damien, Trevor Huddleston,
Jackie Pullinger, Dr Barnardo

RMEP

RELIGIOUS AND MORAL EDUCATION PRESS

Religious and Moral Education Press
An imprint of SCM-Canterbury Press Ltd
a division of Hymns Ancient & Modern Ltd
St Mary's Works, St Mary's Plain
Norwich, Norfolk NR3 3BH

Individual stories first published as separate volumes in the Faith in Action Series:

Free at Last © 1980 R. J. Owen
Island of No Return © 1978 Geoffrey Hanks
I Wish He Was Black © 1978 R. J. Owen
City of Darkness © 1984 Geoffrey Hanks
A Home for All Children © 1980 Geoffrey Hanks

First published in this edition 1991

Reprinted 1994, 1996, 1999

Printed in Great Britain by Polestar Wheatons Ltd, Exeter,
for Religious and Moral Education Press, Norwich

ISBN 0 900274 18 2

CONTENTS

ACKNOWLEDGEMENTS

Photographs are reproduced by courtesy of:
Associated Press Ltd (p.21)
Barnardo Photo Library (pp.92, 98, 101, 106)
International Defence and Aid Fund (pp.53, 54)
Pixfeatures (p.9)
Popperfoto (pp.14, 17, 19)
Jackie Pullinger (pp.70, 81, 88)
South China Morning Post (pp.69, 75, 77, 83)
U.S.P.G. (pp.59, 60)

Cover illustration by Jim Lester

FREE AT LAST

The story of Martin Luther King

R. J. Owen

A black man took his son out to buy him a new pair of shoes. They went into an empty shoe shop and sat down in the front row of seats. A white shop assistant came up to them.

"If you'll move to the seats at the back, I'll be glad to help you."

"There's nothing wrong with these seats," replied the black man.

"You'll have to move. I can't serve you here," continued the shop assistant.

The black man saw no point in moving to other seats when nobody else was in the shop. Anyway, he did not like the idea of people having to sit in special chairs simply because of the colour of their skin.

"We'll either buy shoes sitting here, or we won't buy shoes at all."

"I can't serve you here," repeated the assistant.

Father and son walked out of the shop. The son was Martin Luther King.

Kept apart

As a child Martin lived a comfortable life. His family were quite well off. He and his brother and sister always had enough to eat, good clothes to wear and a nice home.

There was only one thing wrong for Martin. He was black and he lived in a city where most white people thought black people were not as good as white ones. It was the city of Atlanta, in the southern part of the United States.

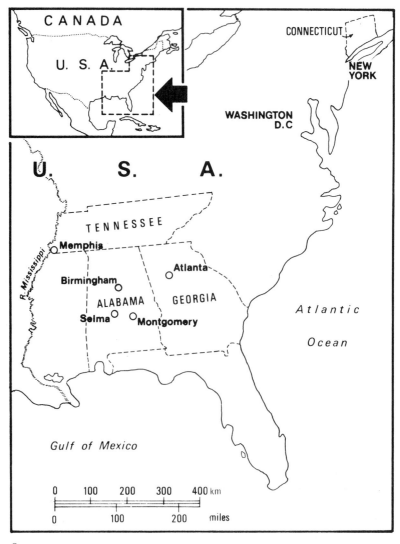

Martin was just six years old when he first learned how hard life could be for black people. Until then, his two best friends were white boys who lived nearby. They played together almost every day. However, when they were old enough to go to school, his best friends went to the school for white children. Martin had to go to the one for black children. His friends' mother kept telling him that they could not play together any more.

Martin could not understand it. He had done nothing wrong. He asked his own mother about it. Mrs King told her son all about the history of the black people in the United States. She told him about how they had been slaves and that some white people still looked down on black people and kept away from them. Mrs King tried to explain why there were many schools, cafés, cinemas, and even churches that black people could not enter. They were only for the use of white people.

"Don't let it make you feel you're not as good as white people," said Martin's mother. "You're just as good as anyone else, and don't you forget it."

Martin's father was also not afraid to stand up for himself. Once, when Martin was being driven in a car by his father, a policeman stopped them. "Boy, show me your licence!" the policeman said to Mr King. That was the way many white people spoke to black people, even if they were grown men.

Mr King pointed to Martin. "Do you see this child here? He's a boy. I'm a man."

The policeman booked him. A black man was not allowed to answer back a white policeman, although the policeman could be as rude as he liked to him!

When he was fifteen years old Martin decided to find out for himself what it was like to live as an ordinary poor black person in the south of the United States. During his long summer holiday from school he took two jobs. The first one was loading and unloading parcels and goods for a railway. The second was working on the loading platform of a firm which made mattresses for beds.

The work was hard. He was able to talk to poor black people and learn about their needs. He noticed that when black people and white people were doing the same job, the whites always got paid more.

He found out what it was like to work under a white boss. The foreman at the railway, for example, never called him by his name. He just shouted out "nigger" when he wanted him. Martin felt sure that, when he was older, he would spend a lot more time trying to get better conditions for black people.

His life's work

During his next summer holiday from school Martin worked in some tobacco fields in Connecticut. While he was there, he was asked by some of the workers to pray with them. They felt he could help them with their problems. From then on, Martin felt a stronger and stronger urge within him to be a minister of a church. He believed it was God's way of telling him that that was what He wanted.

His father was the minister of a large church in Atlanta. Religion, therefore, had always played an important part in Martin's life. He could remember and recite bits from the Bible before he was five years old. When he was only six he used to sing hymns from memory.

He liked to listen to church ministers preaching long before he was old enough to understand what they were saying. Once, when he was about ten, he said to his father, "That man had some big words, Dad. When I grow up, I'm going to get me some big words."

Now, as a teenager, Martin was a pupil at Morehouse College. In the United States such colleges are for teenagers. They are like our secondary schools, except that they are usually much bigger. Morehouse College had over 7000 pupils and was the best college for black students in America.

The head teacher was a man called Dr Mays. He was not a medical doctor but a church minister. When he preached he often talked about being fair to others, and about people being equal. Martin was able to see in this man both Christian faith and real concern for other people.

Martin now believed that he must help people. He wanted to solve the problems they faced in their daily lives, as well as helping them to understand the teachings of Jesus. That is why, later on, his sermons were usually about making life on earth better, as well as about God. He believed that God is a good person who fights against evil things in the world.

So when he was seventeen Martin decided that he would become a church minister. In 1948 he went to a college for those who wanted to become a minister.

It was while he was at the college that Martin first became interested in the teachings of a great Indian man, Mahatma Gandhi. Gandhi lived earlier this century. At the time, Britain ruled India. Gandhi wanted India to be free of British rule. Yet he did not believe in using violence to get rid of the British. He believed in peaceful protest, using methods like marches and strikes. Gandhi urged his followers to break unfair laws, but always to be polite and peaceful. These ideas appealed to Martin. He thought he might one day use them to get equal rights for black people in the United States.

When he had finished his training he became the minister of a Baptist church in Montgomery, Alabama.

The division between blacks and whites was very clear in Montgomery. For example, the front seats on all buses were kept for white passengers only. Even if there was nobody sitting in them and the rear seats were full, black people had to stand at the back. If the front seats were full, black people in the rear had to get up and give their seats to any white person who got on.

Black passengers had to pay their fare at the front of the bus, get off, and walk to the rear door to get on the bus. Sometimes, after they had paid their fare, the bus would be driven off without giving them time to reach the rear door. The white drivers thought this was a great joke.

On 1 December 1955 a black woman, called Mrs Rosa Parks, got on a crowded bus. She had spent a tiring day working and shopping. She found a seat at the beginning of the black passenger section. At the next stop some white people got on. The bus-driver ordered Mrs Parks to get up and give her seat to a white man. She refused. As she said later, "I was just plain tired, and my feet hurt."

The driver called a policeman, who arrested her.

The bus boycott

A number of black church ministers and leaders in Montgomery met to discuss the matter. They wanted to organise a protest. It was agreed to call on all black people not to use the buses on Monday, 5 December. This was called a "bus boycott". On the Sunday before, in every black church, ministers appealed from their pulpits for the people to support the bus boycott.

The first bus on that Monday morning passed Martin's house at about six o'clock. Martin and his wife got up early. Martin was drinking a cup of coffee in the kitchen when it happened.

"Martin, Martin, come quickly!" his wife shouted from the living-room.

Martin rushed in.

"Look, it's empty!" she exclaimed, pointing to the passing bus.

One bus after another went by. All were empty, except for one or two white passengers. It was the same all over the city. The bus boycott was working. For the first time, American black people had united to protest against the unfair way they were being treated. Even though some of them had to walk long distances, the black people refused to use the buses.

The leaders of the bus boycott held a meeting. They decided to call themselves the M.I.A. – the Montgomery Improvement Association. Martin was elected president. They also decided that the bus boycott would go on until the owners of the bus company changed their unfair rules. The bus boycott would cost the owners a lot of money.

That same evening thousands of black people attended a meeting called by the M.I.A. Martin, as president, was to be the main speaker. He had little time to prepare for it. Newspaper reporters and television cameras would be there. He felt nervous. He was not sure what he would say. He decided to pray for guidance.

"Lord, calm me down. Be with me now when I need your help more than ever. Help me to say the right things."

God answered Martin's prayer. After the thousands of people had sung the hymn "Onward! Christian Soldiers", prayed and heard a reading from the Bible, Martin spoke. He told the story of Mrs Parks. He listed some of the ways in which black people were suffering. Then he said:

"We're here this evening to say to those who have treated us wrong for so long, we're tired. Tired of being kept apart. Tired of being shamed. Tired of being kicked about."

Everyone cheered.

"We have to protest," continued Martin. "We've been patient, but we come here tonight to be saved from that patience that makes us patient with anything less than freedom and fairness."

Everyone clapped.

"But," went on Martin, "we must not be violent. Don't force people not to ride on the buses. Our actions must be guided by our Christian faith. Remember the words of Jesus: 'Love your enemies. Bless them that curse you. Pray for them that use you badly.' "

Everyone clapped and cheered.

The bus boycott went on. This was how Martin began trying to get better conditions for black people in the United States. It became known as the Civil Rights movement.

In the middle of one night Martin was wakened by the telephone ringing. He got up and picked up the receiver.

"Listen, nigger," yelled an angry voice, "we've taken all we want from you. Before next week you'll be sorry you ever came to Montgomery."

It was just one of the many horrible telephone calls that Martin and his wife received. He felt he simply could not take any more. With his head in his hands, Martin prayed aloud to God: "Lord, I'm taking a stand for what I believe is right. But I've had enough. I can't face it alone any more."

At that moment Martin sensed that God was with him. He could not explain it. He could only feel it. Inside his mind a voice was saying, "Stand up for what's right. Stand up for truth. God will be at your side for ever." It was strange, but so real. Martin got up, sure that God would give him the courage to go on. He was ready to face anything now.

In the days that followed, Martin had to face many difficult times. Many threatening telephone calls were made to him. Terrible letters came by every post. One read: "This isn't a

Martin Luther King with his family

threat but a promise – your head will be blown off, sure as Christ made green apples!"

One evening Martin was speaking at a meeting. Suddenly he noticed that some people were rushing about, looking worried.

"What's happened?" he asked a friend. His friend, Ralph, did not answer.

"Ralph, you must tell me," said Martin.

"Your house has been bombed."

Martin thought of his wife and young baby. "Are Coretta and the baby all right?"

"We're checking on that now. We think so."

His family were indeed safe, but part of the house was badly damaged. Someone had thrown a bomb into the porch. The porch had been split into two. Windows had been blown into the rooms. Broken glass covered the floors. Light bulbs were smashed. The place was a real mess. Martin rushed over to his wife. "Thank God you and the baby are all right," he said.

Groups of black people, angry at the bombing of their leader's home, were gathering outside. Many carried guns. Policemen were stopping people getting too near Martin's wrecked house. A policeman held back one black man who yelled, "You got your gun. I got mine. Let's shoot it out!"

Black boys were armed with broken bottles. Some of the older black people started insulting the police. They yelled and booed. The police began to threaten the black crowd. Trouble could have flared up at any moment.

Martin went out to talk to them all. When they saw him, everyone went quiet. In a calm voice he said, "My wife and my baby are all right. I want you to go home and put down your weapons."

One black man shouted out, "Aw right, Reverend, if you say so. But ah still thinks we oughta kill a few of 'em!"

"We can't solve anything by violence," Martin went on. "We must meet hate with love. Remember, if I am stopped, this movement will not stop. For God is with this movement."

After that, the crowd began to thin out. People went back to their homes. A white policeman was heard to mutter, "If it hadn't been for that nigger preacher, we'd all be dead."

Success and suffering

The bus boycott went on for over a year. Then, at the end of 1956, the United States Supreme Court made a decision. Keeping black people and white people apart on buses was against the law of the country. Black people were, of course, very happy at the decision. The bus boycott was called off. Most white people accepted the change.

Some, however, were very angry. A few even promised that black people's blood would run in the streets if they tried to sit in the front seats of buses. One letter to Martin threatened that fifty black people's houses would be burnt down, including his, if any black person sat near white passengers. On some nights, buses were stoned. Black people were dragged off buses and beaten up. One woman, who was expecting a baby, was shot in the leg. Several black people's churches and the homes of two of Martin's friends were bombed. A pile of fourteen sticks of dynamite was found just in time on the doorstep of Martin's home.

However, despite all this, the bus boycott had been a success. Black people now had the law on their side. So in 1957 Martin and others began to protest for other rights. They wanted black people to be treated as equals at all times and in all places. On 17 May 37 000 people, black and white, took part in a Freedom March in Washington. Martin spoke to the huge crowd. He demanded that every black person, like every white one, should have the right to vote.

At that time each person who wanted to vote had to pass a test. They had to read a few sentences from a book and then explain what they had read. It was then up to the person testing them to pass or fail them. This was really a crafty way of stopping most black people from being able to vote. Many of them had never been given a good education and, in any case, the test was often not fairly done. The right to vote was what Martin wanted to fight for next.

One day, the following year, Martin was standing in a corridor outside a court-room when a policeman came up to him.

"Move away from here! Move on!"

"I'm waiting to see my lawyer," replied Martin.

"If you don't get the hell out of here you're going to *need* a lawyer," snarled the policeman.

"I'm doing no harm. I'm breaking no law. I'm waiting to see my lawyer. He won't be long."

"Boy, you done it now," shouted the policeman angrily.

Another policeman came over. The two of them grabbed Martin, twisted his arms behind his back and pushed him down some stairs.

Martin was kicked and beaten up. He was charged with not obeying a policeman. Two weeks later he was in court. He was found guilty and given the choice of paying a fine of $10 or going to prison for fourteen days.

"Your Honour," said Martin, "I cannot pay a fine for an act that I did not do. I was about to go into a court-room when two policemen pushed, twisted, choked and kicked me. I did nothing to deserve being treated like that. The black man can no longer silently suffer cruelty from the police. We cannot do so because of what we read in the Bible. We're commanded to resist evil by the God who made us all."

Martin was ready to go to jail. However, the police chief

did not want people to feel sorry for Martin or to think badly of the police. So he paid Martin's fine himself! He said it was "to save the taxpayers the cost of feeding King for fourteen days".

Stabbed

In September 1958 Martin's first book was published. He went to many bookshops to sign his name in copies of his book. One day he went to a bookshop in Harlem, the Negro part of New York. He was signing his name in a copy of his book when a black woman walked up to him.

"Are you Dr King?"

"Yes, I am."

"Luther King, I've been after you for five years."

There was a flash of steel as the woman pulled a knife from her clothing. She plunged it into Martin's chest.

The knife was still sticking in his chest when he was taken to hospital. It was touch-and-go whether Martin would live. The point of the knife was so near his heart that the head surgeon said later, "If he had sneezed he would have died straight away." In order to get the knife out of his chest, two of his ribs had to be removed.

The woman who had stabbed Martin was called Mrs Curry. She was quite mad. She kept saying that Church ministers had caused her a lot of trouble. She was sent to a mental hospital.

Slowly Martin got better. He and his wife felt that God had a purpose in all this. Perhaps it was a test of their faith: Perhaps it was to force Martin to rest and take things quietly for a time. Perhaps it was to help the Civil Rights movement gain more sympathy and support from white people. Perhaps it was to prepare them for something that was still to come. Certainly, believing in God helped Martin to be calm during this time of suffering.

"Sit-ins" and "freedom rides"

In 1960 Martin decided to give up being minister at the Baptist church in Montgomery. He wanted to give more time to the Civil Rights movement. Its headquarters was in Atlanta, so Martin became joint minister at his father's church in Atlanta.

It was in 1960 that the "sit-in" was used as a form of protest by American Negroes. Whites who thought blacks were being treated unfairly joined with blacks in taking action. Together they would "sit in" at cafés and lunch counters in big city shops, where blacks and whites were supposed to be kept apart and be served in different areas. It was during these sit-ins that the song "We Shall Overcome" first became popular. It became the song of the Civil Rights movement.

Many suffered for what they did. They had their hair pulled. They were burnt with cigarette-ends. They were beaten up. Many were arrested, including Martin. He was in jail three times during 1960 and 1961.

Martin Luther King and his friend Ralph Abernathy being arrested after trying to enter a restaurant where Negroes were refused service

Most sit-ins were a success. Hundreds of cafés and shops stopped keeping black and white customers apart.

However, some parts of the United States still had buses in which black people and white people could not sit together. So in 1961 the "freedom rides" started. Groups of young people, both black and white, would get on buses going from one state to another. They would sit together, both on the buses and in the cafés along the way.

Once, in Montgomery, a mob of 300 angry whites formed a circle round a bus as it stopped. The first "freedom rider" to get off was a white man.

"Kill the nigger-loving son of a bitch!" screamed a woman.

Men rushed in and beat the young man until he passed out and fell to the ground. He lay in the street for an hour before an ambulance could get to him.

At Anniston, Alabama, a bus was blown up with a fire-bomb. As the "freedom riders" staggered from the blazing bus, they were beaten with iron bars.

One of the places where black people were treated worst was Birmingham, Alabama. In 1963 Martin and the Civil Rights movement decided to protest there. In April sit-ins and protest marches were held. Within a week nearly 500 black people had been arrested. On Good Friday Martin led a march and was arrested too. He was in jail for eight days.

Shortly afterwards a thousand teenagers were arrested for taking part in a youth march. On the following day another thousand children and teenagers marched. Fire-hoses were turned on them. Children were knocked flat, their clothes soaked and ripped. Police dogs were let off their leads and ran wild. They bit first one child, then another. Some of the older black people could not stand by and do nothing. They began to throw stones and bottles at the police.

There were pictures in the newspapers and on television of young people flattened by jets of water, beaten up by police and bitten by dogs. It caused a storm of angry letters and telegrams to the President of the United States – John F. Kennedy.

The President helps

The President sent Burke Marshall, who was Assistant Attorney-General in charge of Civil Rights, to Birmingham to bring about peace. Peace came. Shops stopped serving blacks and whites in separate places. There were to be more jobs open to black people. All charges against the marchers were dropped. Regular meetings were to be held between black and white leaders.

Then, in August 1963, Martin led a march on Washington for "jobs and freedom". About a quarter of a million people – white as well as black – took part in the march. At the Lincoln Memorial Martin spoke to the vast crowd.

"I have a dream that my four little children will one day live in a nation where they will not be judged by the colour of their skin, but by the sort of persons they are.

"I have a dream that one day . . . all of God's children, black men and white men, Jews and Gentiles, Protestants and Catholics, will be able to join hands and sing in the words of the black people's old song, 'Free at last, free at last, thank God Almighty, we are free at last'."

The march showed America that all blacks and very many whites now believed that everyone was equal, whatever their race or colour.

Some whites, however, still thought that blacks should not be treated the same as themselves. Less than three weeks after the Washington march someone put a bomb in a church in Birmingham. It went off while the Sunday school was being held. Four young black girls were killed.

Later in 1963 President Kennedy was murdered. Martin told his wife, "This is what's going to happen to me also."

The President of the United States, John F. Kennedy

Martin knew he had enemies. He knew he might be shot at or stabbed at any time.

In 1964 the F.B.I. (Federal Bureau of Investigation), the American detective organisation, warned Martin to be careful. It had found out that the Ku-Klux-Klan, a secret society of whites who were anti-black, were trying to hire a "hit man" to kill Martin for a fee of $2000.

In January 1965 Martin was standing in the entrance hall of a hotel in Selma, Alabama. A white man came up behind him and hit him on the head. Martin had a headache for several days to remind him of the attack. A month later the F.B.I. claimed to have stopped an attempt to kill Martin in Atlanta.

Some black leaders were becoming impatient. They thought that the only way to get justice for the black people in America was to fight for it. Martin did not agree. He was determined to keep to peaceful ways, even when he was attacked.

The right to vote

In the autumn of 1964 Martin was told that he had won the Nobel Peace Prize. This is an award given each year to someone who has done much to encourage peace or to stop violence. Martin went to Norway to receive the prize.

The prize was $54 000 (about £30 000). But Martin did not keep it for himself. He gave it away to several freedom movements and organisations which were trying to get equal rights for black people.

The Civil Rights movement moved to Selma. In February 1965 Martin led a march there calling for all black people to have the right to vote. He was arrested again.

In March another freedom march took place in Selma. State troopers blocked the road. The marchers were ordered

Martin Luther King imprisoned in a cell

to stop. They were given two minutes to turn back. Less than a minute went by before the order was given: "Troopers, forward!" Sixty troopers charged into the unarmed marchers to the cry of "Get those goddam niggers!". Tear-gas grenades were thrown at the marchers. They were beaten with clubs and slashed with whips.

"March, nigger! You wanted to march and now I'm gonna help you," screamed one trooper as he whipped a young boy. Over sixty people were injured by this cruelty.

Yet slowly black people were winning their fight for the right to be treated fairly. In August 1965 the Voting Rights Act was passed. Blacks now had the same rights as whites to vote.

Free at last

Martin was concerned about all aspects of fair treatment. In 1964, for example, he and other Church ministers formed a picket line outside the factory of the Scripto Company in Atlanta. He supported the workers (who were mainly black) who wanted to form a union to try and better their working conditions.

Early in 1967 Martin spoke out against the Vietnam war. American soldiers were fighting with the armies of South Vietnam against North Vietnam. Martin was against American soldiers being in the war for two reasons. First, thousands and thousands of Vietnamese people, both adults and children, were being injured or killed. Second, black families and poor families in America were badly affected by the death and injury of their menfolk. Martin wanted peace and equal rights for everybody at home *and* abroad.

In 1968 Martin went to Memphis, Tennessee. He went to arrange a march in support of dustmen there. They had gone on strike because of the unfair way they were being treated by the new mayor.

Martin stayed in Room 306 of the Lorraine Motel. Opposite the motel was a rather shabby hotel. Here a man calling himself "John Willard" rented Room 5B which overlooked the balcony of Martin's room. This man's real name was James Earl Ray, a white American who hated black people.

This man secretly took up to Room 5B a pair of binoculars, a rifle and a box of bullets. At about six o'clock on the evening of Thursday, 4 April, Martin stepped outside on to the balcony of the motel. He went for a breath of fresh air. Soon he would be going out to speak at a meeting.

From the street outside a friend called up, "It's getting chilly, Dr King. Better take an overcoat with you."

"O.K.," Martin replied, "I will."

Suddenly a shot was fired from the shabby hotel opposite. Martin fell backwards. Blood gushed from a three-inch hole in his neck. His brain was damaged. His spine was broken.

He was rushed to hospital. One hour later he was dead – a victim of the violence that for so many years he had tried to stop.

Mrs King had to break the terrible news to her children. The eldest, Yoki, said, "Mum, I'm not going to cry, because my dad's not really dead. His body's dead but his spirit will never die. I'm going to see him again in heaven." Tears were

Martin Luther King on the balcony of the motel where he was shot the following day

running down her cheeks. Then she added, "Mum, should I hate the man who killed my dad?"

"No, darling," said Mrs King quietly, "your dad wouldn't want you to do that."

President Lyndon B. Johnson made the following Sunday a special day of mourning for Martin throughout the country. Important sports events were cancelled. Many television and radio programmes were changed. Martin's wife received over 150 000 letters, cards and telegrams and gifts of flowers from people all over the world.

Many black people were angry. Yet what they did when they heard of his death was against all that Martin believed in. There were riots in some sixty American cities. On hearing that Martin had been shot dead, one black man promised to kill the first white man he saw. He got out his gun, went out into the street and did exactly what he had promised.

At the time of his death Martin and the Civil Rights movement had done much for black people. To separate blacks from whites had been made illegal. It was against the law to refuse a job or not allow a black person to rent a house simply because of his colour. The right of a black person to vote had been accepted.

Such progress continued after Martin's death. Some black people have been elected to public office. In 1973, for example, one man was elected Mayor of Los Angeles. In 1977 another, Andrew Young, became United States Ambassador to the United Nations.

In his final speech on 3 April 1968, at Memphis, Martin spoke of threats against his life:

"Like anybody, I would like to live a long life. But I'm not concerned about that now. I just want to do God's will."

Several times Martin had said to friends, "I'll never live to be forty. I'll never make it." He was thirty-nine years old when he was murdered.

Two months before he died he had said that, if ever he were killed, he would like people to say that "Martin Luther King tried to give his life serving others".

On his gravestone were written these words:

FREE AT LAST, FREE AT LAST
THANK GOD ALMIGHTY
I'M FREE AT LAST

BIOGRAPHICAL NOTES

Martin Luther King was born on 15 January 1929 in Atlanta, Georgia, in the heart of the American South. Educated at Atlanta University Laboratory High School, Booker T. Washington High School and Morehouse College, he went on to study at Crozer Theological Seminary in Chester, Pennsylvania. Here, in 1951, he obtained a Bachelor of Divinity degree. In 1954 Boston University awarded him the degree of Doctor of Philosophy in systematic theology.

Martin was ordained a Baptist minister in 1947, the same year as he was made assistant pastor at Ebenezer Baptist Church, Atlanta.

On 18 June 1953 he was married to Coretta Scott.

In 1954 he was called to the pastorate of the Dexter Avenue Baptist Church in Montgomery, Alabama, where he ministered until 1960. That year he became co-pastor of Ebenezer Baptist Church.

In 1957 Martin was awarded the National Association for the Advancement of Coloured People's Spingarn Medal. This was given to the person making the greatest contribution in the field of race relations. In 1964 he received the Nobel Peace Prize.

Martin Luther King was murdered on 4 April 1968 in Memphis, Tennessee. He was married, with four children (the eldest aged thirteen), when he was killed. His children are called Yolanda (Yoki), Martin (Marty), Dexter and Bernice (Bunny).

Martin Luther King's books include *Stride towards Freedom*, *Strength to Love* and *Why We Can't Wait* (all published in 1958).

ISLAND OF NO RETURN

The story of Father Damien of Molokai

Geoffrey Hanks

"Right," said the police sergeant. "If he won't give in we'll have to kill him—and the woman as well."

The policeman lifted his rifle and pushed another bullet into the barrel. His men did the same, ready for the word to shoot. Everything was still and silent; no one moved. They waited, to give the man one last chance.

From somewhere the man had found a rifle and ammunition, and was prepared to use it on anyone who came too near. For three days the police had been hunting him. They had pleaded with him to give himself up—and his wife. Each time they had been met with a hail of bullets from the hill-top above them.

At that moment a priest appeared. He was a well-made man, with broad shoulders and a sun-burnt face. Everybody knew Father Damien—"Kamiano" to his people. Perhaps the man would listen to the priest?

"Don't shoot yet," asked the priest. "Let me try to talk to him. I might be able to get him to put his rifle down."

"But he's dangerous, Father," protested the sergeant. "He might kill you."

"Just let me try, anyway," pleaded the priest. "The man is from my church."

"All right," agreed the policeman, "but it's at your own risk."

The priest stepped out from behind the rocks and stood in the open, where he could be seen. Immediately three shots rang out.

"Next time my aim will be better," a voice threatened.

"It is me, your friend Kamiano," shouted Father Damien. "I want to help you."

The priest moved forward so that the marksman could see him better. There was silence—no more shots were fired. Damien began to climb the hill. Soon he came face to face with the man, who pointed his rifle at the priest's chest. His finger rested ready on the trigger. Hiding behind him was his unhappy-looking wife.

The white man wanted to take away his wife, he told the priest. She had not done anything wrong. She was not a criminal. All he wanted was to be left alone. True, his wife had leprosy. But it was the white man who had brought it to Hawaii. Now the white man seemed to want to punish her for it. He could look after her himself, he argued. Why couldn't they let his wife die in peace, instead of taking her away?

For six long hours the two men talked. The priest explained that it was an order from the government. All people suffering from leprosy had to go to Molokai—it was feared the disease could spread. That was why she would have to be sent away.

At last the man gave in. He asked only one thing: to be allowed to go with his wife to Molokai. He wanted to be with her in the last few years of her life.

The sergeant agreed. The couple were taken to the harbour to join the others who had been rounded up. Families were standing together, crying and trying to comfort each other. The police stood some distance away.

The time came to leave. The last "goodbyes" were said. Men and women broke away from the sobbing groups and climbed aboard ship. There were even some children who had not yet caught the disease, going with their parents.

Soon the passengers went below to their cabins. The sails were unfurled and a gentle breeze wafted the ship out of the harbour—and out of sight. They were on their way to the island of Molokai, never to see their loved ones again. Within a few years many of the lepers would be dead.

Father Damien never forgot that scene on the harbour front. The memory of those poor people stayed with him. His thoughts followed them across the sea, and he often remembered them in his prayers.

Missionary at work

Father Damien had been born in Belgium in the year 1840. His parents were poor farmers. From childhood he had been taught to love God and always to live a good Christian life. At the age of eighteen he felt called by God to become a priest in the Catholic Church.

After four years of training, he and two priests were sent to the island of Hawaii. They were to become part of a team of missionaries, serving on the island. They arrived there in March 1864, after a five-month voyage from Europe.

Hawaii is the largest of a group of islands in the middle of the Pacific Ocean. They were discovered by Captain Cook in 1778. From 1810 the islands were ruled by a king. (They were never ruled by Britain, even though the Union Jack forms part of their flag.) In 1898 the islands were taken over by the United States, and in 1959 Hawaii became the fiftieth state of the U.S.A.

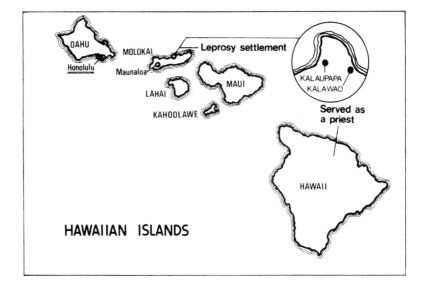

The people of Hawaii were mostly natives. They had bronze skins, large brown eyes and dark-brown or black hair. Gentle, well-mannered and kind to strangers, they lived a simple life and had no desire for riches.

Some of the islanders had become Christians, but many of them still practised their old religions. They trusted in the witch-doctors and offered sacrifices to idols. During the night Damien sometimes heard drums beating as the natives met in secret to dance round their altars.

The priest found that the people spoke English—they had been taught by British missionaries in the mission schools. So Father Damien began to learn the language for himself, and was soon able to use it to talk to the people.

As time went by the islanders began to respect the friendly priest. They knew he worked only for their good, and so they liked him. He awakened in them a new interest in Christianity, and slowly the number of believers began to grow.

Damien was never happy unless he was working. He always had to be doing something. His most important job at first was to build churches, so that he could hold services. He had not been given any money for this work, but was expected to make the best of things. There was plenty of wood in the forest nearby and he was ready to take on any job. By himself, he designed and built six churches on the part of the island where he worked. He cut and shaped the wood, carried it to the sites, put up the framework and covered it with long grass. Each church had a small tower, ready to take a bell.

The natives were amazed at his strength. He could lift by himself a beam of wood that three or four of them had to carry. Long walks over the mountains, plenty of hard work and a simple diet kept him fit.

Yet hardly a day went by without him remembering those unfortunate people who had been sent to Molokai. Some of the people from his churches suffered from leprosy, and were ordered by the police to report for the settlement. He knew the unhappiness their families went through. But he felt so helpless against this terrible disease. If only there was something he could do!

Then, without warning, the chance he had been waiting for arrived. At a meeting held to celebrate the opening of a new church, the Bishop asked for a volunteer to go to Molokai. A priest was needed to look after the settlers. Whoever was chosen would have to stay there for life, he warned.

As he spoke, four young priests sprang to their feet and offered to go.

"Let me go," begged Damien, "I am used to hard work."

"Take care then," said the Bishop. "I will not order anyone to do this work, but I gladly accept your offer."

Everyone knew that the young priest had chosen to die.

Before long, he too would catch leprosy, and then death would not be far away. In those days there was no cure for the disease.

There were no speeches, no words of praise for Damien. Simply a firm handshake and a farewell. There was already a ship in the harbour, taking another group to the island. Without even returning to collect his things or to say "Goodbye", he joined the passengers. One hour after making the offer, he was on his way to Molokai.

The Bishop went with him on the ship, to give him a final few words of advice. In the early hours of the next morning the island came into sight. Boats were lowered to row the new arrivals ashore. The Bishop was able to go with the priest as far as the beach, but was not allowed to land. Standing a short distance away was a sad group of people, suffering from various stages of leprosy.

"So far, my children," the Bishop told them, "you have been left with no one to care for you. Now I have brought someone who will be a father to you all. He loves you so much that he has come to live and die with you."

And so Father Damien stepped ashore at the settlement on Molokai. The Bishop returned to the ship. The priest was left all alone. As he looked around, a voice inside him said, "This is your life's work."

Then he made a promise to himself, that he would never leave these poor people until he also should be taken by the disease.

It was May 1873 when Damien landed on Molokai. He worked there among the lepers for almost sixteen years.

Molokai

The island of Molokai is about sixty kilometres long and eleven kilometres wide. It is covered by mountains, some of them rising over 1500 metres above the sea. Because of this, it is not easy to make a living there, and so few people ever stay.

On the north side of the island there is a low-lying stretch of land, jutting out into the sea. It is cut off from the rest of the island by a huge cliff, over 500 metres high. The cliff makes it almost impossible for people to get on to the main part of the island; certainly it was too steep for any leper to climb.

The leper settlement in Molokai

It was on this stretch of land that the government of Hawaii had opened a settlement for people suffering from leprosy. The first settlers were sent there in 1865, eight years before Father Damien arrived on the island.

The eight hundred people living on the island were housed in two villages. Their huts were poorly made: just a framework of branches covered with either sugar-cane leaves or long grass. A small chapel had been built, but no one had bothered to look after it. There was also a hospital, though it did not have a doctor or even any bandages or medicines.

When the first leprosy sufferers were sent out, they were given a supply of seed and few farming tools. The idea was that they should look after themselves. But with hands and feet rotting away, how could they be expected to grow their own food and provide for themselves?

Supplies soon began to run out. There was no law on the settlement, to make sure that everybody got their fair shares. After a while people began to die—not from leprosy, but from starvation. Those who were strong stole from the weak. With nothing better to do, many of the settlers spent their time in drinking and gambling. Drunkenness became a common sight. Fighting often broke out among the lepers, so that many went about in fear of what might happen to them.

A few people did manage to escape from the island and news of the troubles reached the government. Troops were sent to bring order, but they failed. They were too afraid to go near the lepers, in case they should catch the disease from them.

Then the government decided to give more help to the settlers. Further supplies were sent out, including clothing and a few cattle. A man was sent there to take charge of the work among the lepers, but he did not stay for long. With no one to care for them, the people felt that there was little left in life to hope for.

It was at this point that Father Damien arrived on Molokai. He was thirty-three years old, healthy, strong and able to do the hardest jobs. He was ready for the work he felt God had called him to.

As he strode over the island it was hard to believe his eyes. He had seen leprosy sufferers before, but nothing so awful as these: their bodies were deformed and ugly beyond words. Wounds and sores were left uncovered, and some even had maggots crawling in them.

He reached the village of Kalawao, which was to be his home for the next sixteen years. All the while there was silence—nobody spoke to him or made him welcome. Some, in fact, seemed to resent his presence there. He belonged to the race they believed had caused all their misery.

First he looked round the village, to see what it was like. He found the church and felt that it needed attention. He spent four hours sweeping the floor and repairing the walls. During this time a few of the people stood outside the building, watching him at work. Some brought him small gifts—one brought flowers for the church, and another brought him fruit to eat. He took the gifts from their diseased hands without showing any fear, and thanked them. He had decided that from the beginning he would show them that he was not afraid or put off by their condition.

When he had finished at the church, one of the on-lookers asked him to take a burial service. The priest readily agreed. There was no coffin, and the body had to be wrapped in a mat. It was carried on the shoulders of four friends. The grave was just a shallow ditch. The day before there had been some rain. It had washed the soil away from the graves, leaving the bones of other bodies in view. Damien found the smell sickening, but he forced himself to read the burial service and see that the body was properly buried.

As he walked away from the grave an old woman pulled at his arm. Her son was dying, she said. Would the priest come to see him? Damien went with her. The smell inside her broken-down hut was more than the priest could bear. Several times he had to leave the hut, to get some fresh air.

The dying man was lying on a mat, which was wet from his own filth. His body seemed eaten away by the disease.

Damien knelt down beside the man and took hold of his hands, only to find that most of his fingers were missing. The priest said a prayer for the dying and then waited for the end to come. Before long, the son's eyes flickered and closed for the last time.

By now daylight had gone, and Damien realised that he had been at work for over twelve hours. He had enjoyed only one short break, when he had stopped to eat his fruit. And he had not yet found anywhere to sleep. Although he was not afraid of leprosy, he did not want to sleep in one of the lepers huts. So he chose a tree near the church that he thought might offer him some protection. He spread his mat on the ground and made ready for the night. (This spot under the tree, in fact, was to be his sleeping place for the first few weeks of his life on Molokai.)

Father Damien leaned back against the tree and began to think about his new life. The people needed medical treatment as well as a priest, he thought. They also needed decent homes and a school for the children. And one day he would build a proper church, with a bell tower.

With these thoughts he said his prayers and went to sleep.

Father to lepers

Damien filled every day of his life on Molokai with work. There was always something to be done. He had very little time to himself—the needs of his lepers came first. For their sakes he was doctor, nurse, builder, carpenter, engineer, as well as priest and friend.

Soon after he arrived on Molokai he decided upon a set plan of action for each day. First he always said prayers in his little church, and then he had breakfast. This done, he felt ready for the day.

His most important duty was to visit the sick. He started at the hospital and then went round from hut to hut, seeing to all the lepers. With the help of another white man who also was a leper, he washed the patients and dressed their wounds. It did not matter to him whether a leper was a believer or not, he treated them all alike.

At times he had to act as surgeon. With only a medical book to guide him, he cut off rotting bones and dead limbs. All he used was a knife and a small hatchet; with a few swift blows the job was over. There was no need to put the patient to sleep, because there is no feeling in the diseased limbs.

During the rest of the day there were the usual duties of the priest to be done. Because of the way he cared for them, many of the settlers were won to the faith, and were baptised. Then there were quite a number of weddings to conduct. Even though they might only live together for three or four years at the most, marriage was a comfort to many couples.

And always there were funerals. Between three and four hundred people a year died in the settlement—about one every day. The priest was concerned that everybody should have a decent burial. Whenever possible, Damien made a coffin for the body. He also dug the grave and read the burial service. Later he made a cemetery by fencing off a plot of ground next to the church. He also started a "Coffin Association" to help settlers save up to buy a coffin for themselves.

During his first six years on Molokai Father Damien made most of the coffins, dug the graves and buried about 1600 people. He did it by himself.

Each Sunday the priest held services in the two villages of the settlement. From the beginning he always greeted his people as "We lepers", instead of the usual "My brothers". (He said this to show just how much he wanted to care for them.)

At first few people attended the services, but over the years the numbers began to grow. Many of the settlers came to believe, until the services became quite crowded.

Builder and carpenter

One of his first tasks on the settlement was to lay on a supply of fresh water. Because water had to be carried from a distance, it was very scarce. It was never "wasted" on things like washing and cleaning; it was only for drinking. Even then, many of the lepers actually suffered thirst. They only had the little water they were able to beg from those who could carry it.

Damien decided that somewhere there must be a mountain stream or spring of water that he could tap. A brief search showed that at the end of a valley there was a deep pool of ice-cold water, large enough to supply the settlement. Now all he needed was a supply of pipes and taps. After many letters to the government he at last got his supplies, but no engineer to set it all up.

Not to be put off, he got a group of the fittest of the settlers and started on the work. It took many days before a steady stream of cold water was flowing into the village. Taps were fixed within the reach of every hut. The people were thrilled to find they could now have as much water as they wanted.

From then on, the people had a new respect for this kindly priest.

But Damien was not content to sit back and rest. There were other jobs to be done. Housing in the two settlement villages was so bad that each hut he visited made him feel sick. The huts were poorly built, damp and without fresh air. They were made worse by the people's own dirty habits, so that the smell became unbearable. Yet it was difficult to make the people see the need for better homes and a cleaner way of living.

Then one night the problem was solved for him. A fierce storm blew down nearly all the huts, so new ones *had* to be built. Once more he wrote to the government asking for help. It took some time, but at last several ship-loads of timber arrived at the island. All those able to work set about building new homes.

Many of the settlers had to rely once more on Damien. Some paid others to do the work for them. It is estimated that the priest and his boy-helpers worked on about three hundred of the new cottages.

Each cottage was built on trestles. This raised it above the ground and kept the floor dry. A strong timber frame was put up, which was then covered with rough boards

Leper's hut

and painted white. The cottages were placed in rows, and Damien encouraged the settlers to plant a garden. Each house was provided with a small plot of land for vegetables and flowers.

By now Father Damien had his own home as well. It had one room and measured five metres by three metres. It was close by the church—and the cemetery!

Damien did all that he could to make the people forget that they were "outcasts". He helped them to become real people again, so that they could hold their heads up high. He gave them self-respect.

Slowly life in the settlement began to change. It was not just the new homes or the water supply. It was something in the people. They had begun to realise that there was someone who loved them, who cared about what happened to them. This was the *real* change that was going on.

Leprosy

For thousands of years people have been afraid of leprosy. They thought that it could be caught just by mixing with people who already had the disease. They knew that in most cases it ended in a terrible death. So people with leprosy were sent away from their homes and villages, to live out in the open.

We now know much more about leprosy. Medical research tells us that it is not an easy disease to catch. It is mainly caught through close contact with a sufferer over a long period. Through use of modern medicine it is often successfully treated and cured.

Leprosy is widespread in hot countries like India, New Guinea, parts of Africa and China. It is very rare in Europe, although it was once quite common. There are about ten million people in the world who suffer from leprosy today.

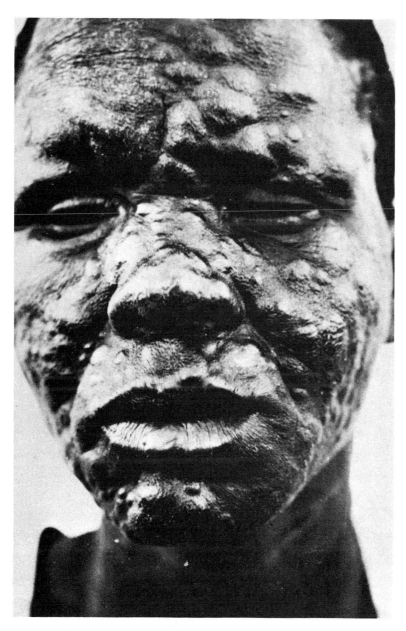

Leprosy sufferer before treatment

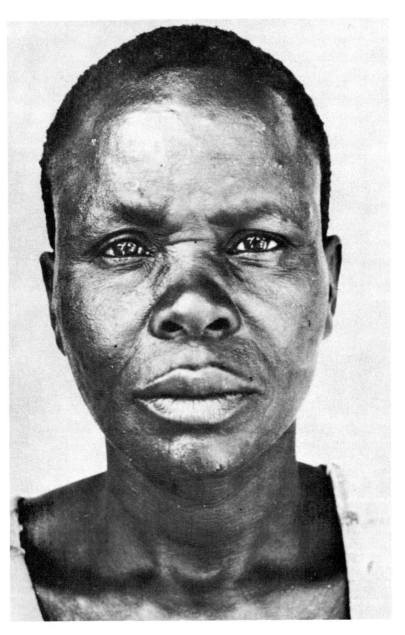

Leprosy sufferer following treatment

Leprosy is a disease of the nerves. It often begins with white patches appearing on the skin. As the nerves die so the sufferer loses feeling. For example, if a leper burns or cuts himself without knowing, he will carry on as if nothing had happened. If the wound is not treated it will often become poisoned. This leads to loss of limbs as the skin and bone become damaged. Usually the fingers and toes are lost and later a hand or foot. Sometimes, without treatment, the leper dies through loss of blood from these injuries.

Leprosy also weakens the muscles, resulting in clawed hands or feet. Fortunately an operation on tendons and bones can sometimes put them right.

In other cases, the disease spreads quickly and large lumps form on the sufferer's face and ears. The disease also attacks and destroys parts of the body, such as the voice box and the nose.

Doctors now know that leprosy does not kill. It is the *results* of the disease that cause death. So people were more afraid of leprosy than they need to have been. In Father Damien's time the only answer was to send the sufferer away, in the hope that the disease would not spread. Today it is possible to cure people and help them live a useful life.

A new happiness

There must have been times when Father Damien wondered whether he would ever finish the work he had set out to do. With no one but a few native helpers, Damien worked for most of the time all alone among the people on the settlement.

He often wrote to the government Board of Health for

supplies, but they seemed unwilling to help. Once, when no supplies came, he went to Honolulu by boat to see what could be done to hurry them along. He argued with the officials, and he even lost his temper with them. They said he should stick to his missionary work and not interfere with what they were trying to do.

As a result of this visit, the government passed a new law. It said that anyone leaving the settlement would be arrested and put in prison: *no one* would be allowed to leave, whatever the reason.

Almost to the end of his life Damien continued to have arguments with the officials. They resented his impatient outbursts—he was angry with their lack of understanding.

After seven long years of working alone another priest came to help. But Father Damien was not always easy to work with; he was a hard man and quick to lose his temper (though never with his leper friends). The new priest left after a year. The next helper stayed two years before leaving. The third, an American, got on famously with Damien—and he stayed on the island forty-four years!

Later on six more helpers arrived at the settlement. They came to work at the hospital, to look after the most urgent cases.

One of the saddest problems Father Damien faced was that of the many children at the settlement whose parents had died. At first the priest persuaded some of the settlers to give the children a home. After three years on the island, Damien built a house to shelter a group of homeless girls. He appointed a woman as cook, cleaner and mother. The government made a small grant towards their keep, by way of a weekly ration of meat.

Later a home was opened, to care for about forty boys. It was to be several years, however, before the home could be staffed by nurses and school teachers.

Father Damien with young boys of the colony

Meanwhile Damien had not forgotten the children's education. When he had the chance, he used to hold lessons in the open air. Before long he managed to build a small school, and then another one a few years later.

He also rebuilt the hospital that he found when he first arrived. Somehow he was able to get a few beds for the patients. He persuaded some of the more healthy settlers to act as nurses. Then to his great joy a doctor arrived to take charge of the hospital. The doctor brought new medicines that could control leprosy, even though there was still no cure.

The priest did all he could to encourage the Hawaiians' love of music. The Bishop had some musical instruments sent out to them, and Damien formed a number of choirs. Each evening crowds gathered under the trees near the church, to make music. Sometimes new songs and hymns were composed, either about their island or about their new faith.

Church festivals were always happy occasions. For weeks before, everybody was busy making preparations. People collected flowers and made themselves new clothes. The choirs put in extra practices. And when the day came, everyone turned out to enjoy themselves.

As the years went by, Father Damien's efforts began to show results. The lepers started to take a new interest in life. They learned to laugh and they began to forget their miseries a little. As they listened to the gospel that Damien preached, they began to follow the Master that he served. They found a new way of living.

Gently drawn towards the grave

Father Damien always knew that one day he too would catch leprosy. He was not afraid of the disease, nor was he afraid of dying. But when leprosy attacked him, it still came as a shock.

One evening, feeling rather unwell, he boiled some water for a foot-bath. Without thinking, he dipped both his feet into the boiling water. He rested them in the water for some while. He only guessed what was happening when he saw blisters appearing on his feet. Then he realised he could not feel any pain. He was a victim of leprosy!

At first the priest told no one, but other signs soon followed: more white patches, on his cheek and ear; the loss of his eyebrows. Later small lumps began to appear on his face.

When the Bishop learned of his illness, he ordered Damien back to Honolulu for treatment. The priest obeyed, not happy at the thought of leaving his lepers. For two weeks he was in hospital and there seemed to be an improvement. He could not stay idle for long, however, and so he returned to Molokai.

Meanwhile, news of his illness had reached the newspapers. The sacrifice that Damien had made was told round the world. Money and gifts began pouring in, to

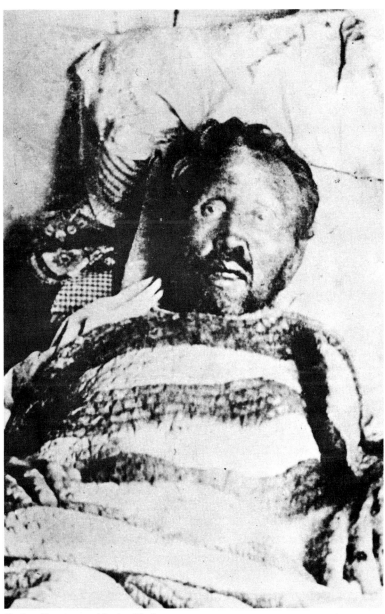

Father Damien on his deathbed

support the work. A sum of two thousand pounds, for example, was collected by a clergyman from Camberwell, London, for the lepers.

But Damien's body was slowly wasting away. This once strong man was weakening every day. He carried on with his work as well as he could—building, visiting the sick and even burying the dead. When his legs became crippled he was taken about in a horse-drawn cart. He was bright and cheerful as usual.

"Look at my hands," he said. "All the wounds are healing and the crust is becoming black—a sign of death."

He wrote to his brother at this time, "I am quite happy and contented. Although seriously ill, all I want is to do the will of God."

From then on he thought only of preparing for death. He made arrangements for leaving the few things he had to his close friends. He asked that he should be buried under the tree where he had first slept on the island.

"How happy I am to have given all to the Lord," he remarked. "Now I die poor, having nothing of my own."

All this time Damien was laid on a mattress on the ground at the door of his hut. He did not own any bed-clothes or even a bed. He had given all his money to help his people.

A crowd gathered round his hut, waiting for news of their priest. As Damien's life began to slip away, he was given Holy Communion for the last time. A short while before the end came, a rather wonderful thing happened— all signs of leprosy left his face! The lumps were no longer there. His end came peacefully, as though he had fallen asleep. It was April 1889.

In a way, Father Damien's death was more important than his life. When he died the news of what he had done on Molokai spread round the world. For the first time people began to pay attention to reports about leprosy. Conditions in India, Africa and China became headline news. People began to *do* something for those who suffered.

At the same time that Father Damien went to Molokai a similar work was going on in India. To support the efforts of a man called Wellesley Bailey, the Mission to Lepers was started in 1874.

In England, the Prince of Wales, later to be King Edward VII, was very moved by Father Damien's sacrifice. With the Prince's help, a large cross from the people of Britain was set up on Molokai to remember the priest's work. Underneath were some words from the Bible:

"Greater love hath no man than this, that a man lay down his life for his friends."

Later, the King of Belgium asked for Father Damien's remains to be brought back to his home country. In 1936 the body was carried back to Belgium by a warship. Waiting at the harbour was the King and an Archbishop, to pay their last respects to the priest of the Great Heart.

BIOGRAPHICAL NOTES

Father Damien was born Joseph De Veuster, 3 January 1840, in the village of Tremeloo, in Belgium. His parents were of peasant stock and ran a small farm. They were devout Catholics and brought up their six children to love God. Joseph's father planned that his youngest son should become a merchant, and sent him to school to gain a commercial education. At the age of eighteen, however, Joseph attended a Mission, through which he felt called by God to become a priest. His father was at first reluctant, but later agreed. In January 1859 Joseph joined his older brother Pamphile as a member of the Congregation of the Sacred Hearts of Jesus and Mary, known sometimes as the Picpus Fathers, and took the religious name of Damien.

Pamphile De Veuster was due to go out to the South Seas as a missionary. Because of illness, however, he was unable to accept the call. Joseph persuaded his Superior to allow him to take his brother's place. Although not yet an ordained priest, he was given permission. He sailed from Bremerhaven, Germany, in October 1863, and reached Hawaii in March the following year. At Whitsuntide of that year, Joseph De Veuster was ordained priest and became Father Damien.

He spent nine years as a parish priest on the island of Hawaii, before volunteering for the leprosy settlement on Molokai in May 1873.

He died on 15 April 1889. His body was reinterred in Belgium in 1936.

I WISH HE WAS BLACK

The story of Trevor Huddleston

R. J. Owen

Two boys bumped into each other in the school corridor. They glared at each other.

"Watch where yer goin', you stupid wog!" yelled one.

"It was your fault, whitey!" answered the other.

"Lookin' for a fight, coon?"

The talking stopped. The lads pushed each other. Other pupils gathered round. Punches were thrown. Soon the two boys were wrestling on the corridor floor.

Things like that happen every day, perhaps even at your school. Children and young people insult one another simply because they have different coloured skins. That's bad enough, but in some countries, such as South Africa, it is far worse. There, even some of the laws for black people are different from those for whites!

For example, in South Africa black people from the age of sixteen have to have a pass in order to travel and to work. A pass is issued by the Government. It is a card which contains the person's photograph, name, tax details and the area within which he is allowed to travel.

Each African must always carry his pass with him. Without it, he can be arrested and put in prison. Yet white people do not need to have a pass.

I Wish He Was Black

For many years now, Trevor Huddleston has been trying to show people how unfair such laws are. He has also been helping those who suffer from living under these laws.

Trevor Huddleston was born in Bedford, a town about fifty miles north-west of London, in 1913. He went to school in Sussex and then to Oxford University. While he was at Oxford, he heard a priest give a talk about the terrible conditions in which some people were living in London. He felt sorry for these people.

During part of his university holidays, Trevor worked on a farm in Kent, helping to harvest the crop of hops. Other students worked with him, and there were also many families from London. Families often did this in the summer. It was a way of having a holiday in the country and earning some money at the same time. But they had to work very hard — even the children.

These families were very poor. Some were without a father at all, while in others the father could not get a regular job. In the 1930s jobs were usually very difficult to get unless you were clever or came from a well-to-do family. Meeting these people made Trevor want to help them, and other families like them.

He thought about working among poor people when he left university. However, after leaving Oxford, he first spent six months visiting India, Ceylon and Burma. He went there because his father and grandfather had worked in India, and he wanted to see this and the other countries for himself.

In these places too, travelling around, he saw lots of poor and starving men, women and children. He still hoped that perhaps one day he would be able to do something for such people.

When he returned from India Trevor attended a special college for young men who want to become priests. He felt that this was the way to make sure of putting himself in God's hands.

The college was in the pretty countryside of Somerset. It was an area quite different from busy London or dusty India. He studied hard and in 1937 became a priest of the Church of England.

He worked as a priest in a parish in Swindon, Wiltshire, but after only two years he left. He believed that God wanted him to become a monk. Monks usually live together in a large building called a monastery. They spend much time worshipping God and studying the Bible. But they also do many ordinary jobs, keeping the monastery clean and tidy and working in its vegetable and fruit gardens.

Some monks, however, live in the monastery but work in a nearby town or village. They might be teachers, playgroup leaders, youth club leaders or do any job which means helping ordinary people. All the money they earn goes to the monastery, not to them.

Trevor joined a group of monks called the Community of the Resurrection, based at Mirfield, near Leeds. It was a big decision for him to take, and it could not have been an easy one. He had to make three promises. First, he promised to give up all money and possessions. Second, he promised not to get married. Third, he promised to go wherever the Community sent him.

Sophiatown

In 1943 the Community sent Trevor out to South Africa. He was to look after the Community's school and church in Sophiatown. Sophiatown is a small African town on the edge of a very large city called Johannesburg.

White people live in the rich, modern city with its fine houses, large offices and pleasant shops. Black people usually

Living conditions: inside a house in an African township.

have to live in the slum area of Sophiatown with its closely packed, crowded little houses and much sickness and disease.

For thirteen years Trevor was the priest at the Church of Christ the King in Sophiatown. He saw how "apartheid" (say it as if it was spelt "apart-hate") worked.

Apartheid is a word meaning "segregation" — that is to say, the separating of groups of people from each other. In South Africa the law says that white people and black people must live in separate areas, travel in different buses, work in different places and learn in different schools. Also, a black person is not allowed to marry a white one.

The government in South Africa believe in apartheid.

A police baton charge into a crowd of black Africans.

They think that keeping apart people of different races and colours is the right thing to do.

White people have been in South Africa for about 350 years. The first white people came from Holland. Then in about 1820 some British settlers arrived. There was much fighting as the Dutch and British each tried to take over the whole country for themselves. The white people wanted to rule it so that they could become rich by digging for the gold and diamonds that were, and are still, to be found there.

There have always been fewer whites than blacks in South Africa. Perhaps this explains why the white government keep apartheid. They know that if the non-whites were given the same rights as the whites, the black people would take over the country again. Then the whites would lose a lot of power and a lot of money.

Trevor thought how unfair and cruel it was to treat people badly just because they were black.

One of his friends in Sophiatown was called Jacob

Ledwaba. One night, just before Easter, Jacob was arrested for being out without his pass. For twenty-four hours he was kept in a cell at the local police station. While he was there, he was kicked in the stomach by policemen who were questioning him.

As a result of the injuries he received, he died. Jacob was only a young man. He left a widow and a month-old baby. He had been a bit careless, and because he was black it cost him his life.

African children are also in great danger if they forget to carry with them their special school pass. Even if a school-boy does have one with him, he can still be picked upon and beaten.

Trevor knew a boy called Jonas. Jonas was home from school for his summer holidays. One morning he was arrested and charged with being a tramp! Black lads who sit in the same place day after day or lazily kick a tin-can around as they walk slowly about, because they have nothing better to do, risk the anger of white police. So it was with Jonas.

As soon as Trevor heard that Jonas had been arrested, he set out for the police station. He arrived at about tea-time. Jonas was in the yard of the station. He was about to be locked up for the night.

"Jonas, are you all right?" Trevor's concern was real. He knew that the law allowed physical punishment. Some policemen were little more than thugs.

"I'm O.K., Father," replied Jonas. (It is quite common for people in the Church of England and the Roman Catholic Church to call their priest "Father".)

"Did you have your pass with you?" asked Trevor.

"Yes, Father."

"Well, where is it?"

"The police tore it up, and then said I didn't have one."

At that, Trevor walked straight into the police station. Without saying anything he went over to the waste-paper basket and looked inside. Amongst cigarette-ends and other rubbish he found the pass. It was torn into four pieces. Jonas had told the truth.

"What do you think you're doing?"

Trevor looked up. The gruff voice was that of a police sergeant.

"But it's Jonas's," Trevor pointed out.

"It's police property now!" The sergeant was getting angry.

"You said the lad hadn't got a pass, so I can't give you what you say he's never had."

Trevor's clever talking made the sergeant lose his temper. He arrested Trevor! However, a more senior policeman later said sorry to Trevor for the "mistake". Jonas was allowed to go home and the matter was forgotten.

Yet, as Trevor himself says, "For every boy like Jonas whose arrest was reported to me, there are a thousand who have no one to care. There are a thousand for whom a torn-up pass might mean ten days in prison or the loss of a job. And that's the sort of thing which leads lads into crime."

No homes

The government in South Africa were not worried about whether or not black people had somewhere to live. They were only concerned that there were enough blacks to do the hard and dirty jobs.

Few Africans could find jobs in the villages and towns, so they had to move near to the big cities. They were not paid much for what they did, so more and more of them could not afford to rent or build a proper home.

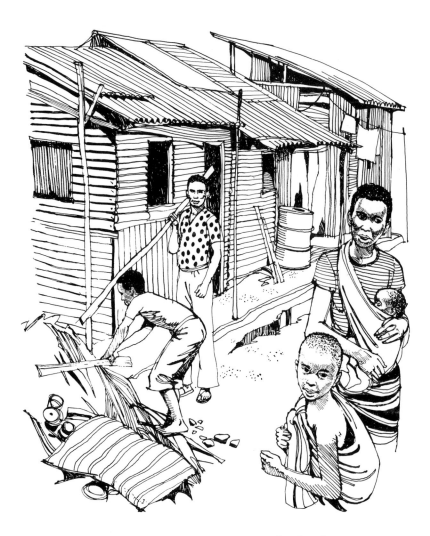

In the mid-1950s Johannesburg had about 40 000 homeless African families. Few of them had any hope of getting a home, even though they worked in the city. These families did the only thing they could — they built corrugated-iron shacks in the yards of other Africans' homes.

The city council, however, ordered all the shacks to be destroyed. If any were not pulled down, the person who owned the land would be taken to court. Trevor Huddleston urged one man, George Ndhlovu, not to destroy the shacks in his back yard. George agreed. What would happen? Would there be a trial?

Meanwhile Trevor went to see the Medical Officer of Health. The man sat behind a broad desk playing with some paper-clips while Trevor explained the problems of the homeless families.

"The position is quite clear," said the Medical Officer. "People have been warned not to have shacks built on their land. George Ndhlovu has taken no notice. These shacks cause extra crowding. It's not healthy to have them."

"Yes, I agree that they become slums," replied Trevor. "But there are thousands of people without a home. Where are they to go?"

"That's nothing to do with me," answered the Medical Officer. "I'm here to make sure the law is carried out."

"But you can't deal with people as if they're things. You can't turn them out into the street in winter without a roof over their heads."

"I tell you, it's nothing to do with me."

Trevor went to see other important people, but got the same reply. Did nobody care?

Then George Ndhlovu was brought to court. He was, of course, found guilty. Just as the judge was about to fine him, a voice was heard at the back of the court. It was the voice of Trevor Huddleston.

"May I say something, Your Worship?"

The judge looked surprised and rather stern. "What is it you wish to say?"

"Simply that it's wrong to punish a man for something that's not his fault but the fault of society."

Apartheid in action: a bench for "Europeans only" in Johannesburg.

The judge was cross. "That's enough! You must sit down. This is a court and you have no right to speak."

"I'm sorry, but I shall not sit down until I have said what I came here to say."

But the judge cleared the court before Trevor could say anything else.

Later, outside in the corridor, the chief judge spoke to Trevor. "I am surprised at you, a minister of religion, making trouble in court."

"As a minister of religion, should I stand by and let people be turned out into the street and do nothing about it?" Trevor replied quietly.

"I warn you, I won't have my judges attacked in this way. . . . "

Yet Trevor knew that so long as he was in South Africa

Apartheid in action: separate stairways for whites and non-whites.

he must fight apartheid and stand up for the rights of the African. After the court case, the city council didn't seem to bother about the shacks any more. Trevor believed it had been worth the fight.

Trevor Huddleston did many things to try to make the life of the Africans easier. The Community ran a small nursery school, and Trevor decided to open it at night for homeless children. Many of the children were becoming ill because of the cold, wintry nights. In the evenings he went to the school to help bath the very young children, then put them to bed.

One night, after he had said prayers with them, a little boy suddenly caught hold of Trevor's hand as he was passing and kissed it. This small act was enough to show Trevor the love which many Africans felt for him. Another time a child said of Trevor, "I wish he was black!"

In nearly every African town there were children starving to death. This was because black people had to buy food at the same prices as white people. Yet a black person was paid only about a tenth as much as a white person for doing the same job!

So Trevor started the African Children's Feeding Scheme. By writing letters to newspapers and asking for money, he was able to set up centres in these towns where every morning a child could get a decent meal for a halfpenny.

The Feeding Scheme continues today because African children are still starving to death. Some white people in South Africa do not know what is going on. Others prefer not to notice and pretend they do not know.

Trevor did not think it was fair that only white people had nice things to enjoy. So he organised the building of a beautiful swimming-pool for the use of Africans. He also arranged for the world-famous violinist, Yehudi Menuhin, as well as other well-known musicians, to play in Sophiatown free of charge. No African is allowed to go to white people's places of entertainment, so the black people had never heard such music and such great musicians before.

One afternoon Hugh, a fourteen-year-old schoolboy, walked into Trevor's office and sat down on the arm of a chair. At first Trevor took no notice. He was used to young children and teenagers coming in and out of his room. Sometimes they wanted to talk. Sometimes they just sat down and read a magazine. Sometimes they asked him questions.

"Father," Hugh began, "I want to learn to play the trumpet."

"Good idea," replied Trevor, "but trumpets cost a lot of money. You'll have to save up for a long time before you can buy one."

"But I love music," Hugh went on, "and I want to prove to my father that I can play the trumpet."

A few weeks later, when Hugh lay ill in bed, Trevor went to a shop which sold trumpets. He bought a second-hand one. He gave it to Hugh, who was very excited. When he was better, the lad practised every day and soon was able to play tunes.

Other boys became interested in learning how to play music. Somehow or other, by buying or borrowing, Trevor got hold of many other musical instruments. Soon he was able to start a teenagers' jazz band in Sophiatown!

One thing Trevor could not do was to change most white men's opinion of black people. There was, for instance, a clever and able young man called David, who was black. Trevor had managed to get him a job in the packing department of a large store. Three weeks later, he went to see him to find out how he was getting on. David told him: "It's all right, Father, except for the white lady. Sometimes when I am shifting boxes I have to move an account sheet or a bill. As soon as I pick it up, the lady yells at me, 'Don't touch that paper! Paperwork is white work. It's not for natives!' "

Back to England

Some white people are brave enough to go against the ideas and laws of the Government, because they believe them to be wrong. Many of these people are Christians. Life is often hard for them. Many people who have dared to speak out are put in prison.

Trevor was not put in prison, but the police did watch him closely. There were police raids where he lived and Trevor's room was searched for anything which might be held against him. The police found nothing. All Trevor did was to ask the policemen if they would like a cup of tea!

A member of the South African Government said that Trevor deserved to be thrown out of the country or strung up from the nearest lamppost as a traitor. Another claimed that in the Middle Ages people like Trevor would have been burned at the stake!

Even some Christians thought he was wrong.

"The Church should not get involved with politics," some said.

"You should obey the Government," others told him.

All this made him sad. Didn't they understand? Didn't they care about the thousands of Africans who were suffering? For Trevor, the issue was clear: apartheid was evil and unchristian and had to be fought.

In 1956 Trevor was called back to England by the Community of the Resurrection. He did not want to go. He did not want to leave behind all the African friends he had come to love. However, seventeen years before, in the Community's church in Mirfield, he had made a promise to obey and go wherever the Community sent him. And so he left.

"To say goodbye to Sophiatown and South Africa was the hardest thing I ever had to do," admits Trevor. "I can feel the ache of it to this day. But it was not my decision and doing what you're told like this brings you peace of mind."

He arrived back in England to find that the *Daily Mirror* had made him "The Man of the Year"! He was famous! Many called him a hero, a great man, a fighter for human rights.

He wrote a book and various newspaper articles, gave talks and was interviewed on radio and television. In this way he was able to draw the attention of people in Britain to what was happening in South Africa.

For four years he lived at the Community's homes in Mirfield and London. However, he also travelled abroad, to places like the United States and the West Indies, speaking on behalf of the black people of South Africa.

Africa again!

Then Trevor was made Bishop of Masasi in Tanganyika (now Tanzania). He could hardly wait to get back to Africa. In September 1960 he left England once again.

Life in Masasi was very different from that in Sophiatown. For one thing, the weather was much hotter. Sophiatown had been noisy and crowded, but Masasi was a quiet and lonely place. Often he travelled around by Land-Rover and slept at night in a mud hut. Once he found a large snake called a cobra under his wardrobe!

One of his main jobs in Masasi was to train Africans to be priests and leaders of their Church, instead of foreigners like himself. He did this partly by teaching them about the Bible, Church history and how to preach. He also took one or two of them with him on his travels and visits all over Masasi. In this way they could see what it was like to be a priest and a bishop.

Trevor noticed how bored some of the young teenagers were. Most of them were not allowed to go to school after they were twelve, for there were not enough teachers and schools. Yet the lads were too young to start farming, which was what most Africans did. There were no cinemas, no sports fields, no television.

Trevor had an idea. Football! He wrote to all his friends in England asking them to send him footballs. The footballs came — and so did teenagers from all over Masasi! Almost every day the Bishop was greeted by "Nataka mpira" (I want a football).

One day, in a village called Marika, Trevor was sitting in the shade having his breakfast. A lad came limping up to him. The boy was on crutches and one of his legs was short and twisted. It seemed he must have had the terrible disease of polio.

"Nataka mpira," said the boy with a grin.

Trevor smiled back. Clearly the crippled boy could not play football, but wanted one for his friends. Trevor found one for him straight away.

Trevor enjoyed his life in Africa, but after almost eight years he was called back to England again. He had been made Bishop of Stepney.

Stepney includes three large London boroughs — Tower Hamlets, Hackney and Islington. It is a part of London where there are people of all races and colours. Trevor seemed the ideal man for the job.

There were many people in Stepney who were in need. There still are — people without a job, people without a decent home, people who are very poor. This is the place where Trevor worked for ten years. He tried to get them better living conditions. He tried to help them with their problems.

In 1978 Trevor was made Bishop of Mauritius, a small island in the Indian Ocean. He continues to fight for what he thinks is right. He puts over the Christian view whenever he can. He says that Christians in this country should be concerned for the black people in South Africa. They should protest, by vote and — where necessary — by more direct action. They ought to show their concern for the hungry world and for fairness in race relations everywhere.

As for Trevor himself, he will go on fighting apartheid until he or apartheid is dead.

BIOGRAPHICAL NOTES

Trevor Huddleston was born in Bedford in 1913. He studied at Christ Church College, Oxford, and at Wells Theological College.

He was ordained as a Church of England priest in 1937. After a brief ministry at St Mark's Church, Swindon, Wiltshire, he entered the Community of the Resurrection.

In 1943 he was sent by the Community to be parish priest at the Church of Christ the King in Sophiatown, an African township on the edge of Johannesburg.

From 1956 to 1958 he was Novice-Master of the Community in Mirfield, and from 1958 to 1960 he was Prior of the Community's London House.

He has been Bishop of Masasi in Tanganyika (1960-68), Bishop of Stepney (1968-78) and Bishop of Mauritius (1978-83).

Trevor Huddleston has frequently appeared in radio and television programmes and has written many newspaper articles. His book, *Naught for Your Comfort*, which was published in 1956, has become a "classic" for those interested in or involved in South Africa and its racial problems and policies.

He is president of the Anti-Apartheid Movement, and in 1982 received the United Nations Gold Medal Award in recognition of his work against apartheid. He now lives with the Community of the Resurrection at Mirfield, West Yorkshire.

CITY OF DARKNESS

The story of Jackie Pullinger

Geoffrey Hanks

It was five o'clock in the morning when the telephone rang. Jackie Pullinger struggled out of bed and reached for the receiver.

"Hello," she muttered wearily.

"You've got to come quickly," a voice said. "There's been a break-in at the club. Everything's in a terrible mess."

Then the caller rang off, but Jackie had recognised the voice of Ah Ping, one of her youth club members.

She dressed quickly and hurried down into the street. Everyone else in Kowloon seemed to be still in bed. There were no buses about, so she ran as fast as she could. Soon she spotted a taxi, and asked the driver to take her to the Walled City. Within minutes she arrived at the club-room.

The damage was worse than she had feared. Benches, table-tennis bats and skateboards had been smashed and the bits thrown around the room. Books had been torn up, and sewage from the open drains in the street had been daubed all over the walls and the floor.

Jackie was so upset by what she saw that she wanted to sit down and cry. She had run the youth club for four years and believed the boys to be her friends. And now this had happened. Feeling angry and let down, she thought of giving up the work.

Then Jackie remembered how Jesus had also been betrayed by His friends. She spent the whole day cleaning up the mess, sobbing, getting ready to open the club again.

In the Walled City

In England, Jackie Pullinger had been a teacher. But she gave up teaching to become a missionary, because she felt that this was what God wanted her to do. Not knowing exactly where to go, she bought a ticket to Japan. When the ship reached Hong Kong, she decided to get off. She had no plans and knew no one in Hong Kong. All she had was about £6, her clothes and her guitar.

"God will show me what to do," she told herself, and waited to see what would happen.

Soon Jackie found a job at a mission school in the Walled City in Kowloon, part of Hong Kong. This is where it all started.

When Jackie first went there, the Walled City was a shanty town. Most people there lived in shacks made of wood, corrugated iron and other waste materials. A whole family often had to eat, sleep and even work in just one room.

The streets of the City were so narrow that hardly any light could get through to the houses, and as there was no electricity, the place was in almost total darkness. There were only four proper toilets in the whole area, and all the rubbish and sewage was thrown into the open drains.

There were said to be over 30 000 people living in the Walled City, an area the size of about six football pitches. In such a place, it was easy to hide. So it became a home for criminals, drug addicts, gamblers and gold smugglers. Anyone trying to escape from the police could find safety here. It was also the home of a large number of homeless boys, many of them thrown out by their parents.

Two views of the Walled City in the 1970s

As the police hardly ever entered the Walled City of Kowloon, it became a sort of no man's land, run by criminals, a centre for all that is worst in the world of crime and vice.

For many years, crime in the Walled City was controlled by two gangs of Triads. The original Triad Society was a group of men who worked secretly to overthrow the Manchus, who had conquered China in the seventeenth century. Today, however, Triads are mainly gangs of men and teenage boys who band together to make a lot of money by controlling crime.

When Jackie arrived in Hong Kong, the top man in the Walled City was a man called Goko. He was said to have several thousand followers. Each gang member promised to follow his "big brother" (the leader of the gang) and became his leader's "little brother", so all the gang members were part of the same family. The brothers were sworn to go to each other's aid if they were in trouble, even at the risk of death.

It was in this place that Jackie found work. Although she could not speak Chinese, she managed to teach the children singing and English! It was five years before she could speak Chinese well. Meanwhile, the children gave her a Chinese name: Poon Siu Jeh, or Miss Poon for short. (In China, the surname comes first, before the other names.)

On Saturday afternoons, Jackie ran a club for boys in the Walled City. They played football, table tennis and darts, and went roller-skating and boating. During the school holidays, Jackie took them camping, too. Later on, as the club became more popular, she opened it up on several evenings during the week as well.

A new beginning

Jackie's main aim was to get people in the Walled City to understand about Jesus, but, despite all her efforts, things did not go well. The youth club was not very successful and no one seemed to want to listen to her. She realised that she would have to put her message across in actions, not just in words.

Jackie began to give people practical help with their problems. She went with the boys to interviews for jobs or school places. If they were taken to court or sent to prison, she stood by them. She visited their homes to see what else she could do for them.

As the news of Jackie's work spread, all kinds of people in the City began to seek her help. They thought of her as a rich westerner and assumed she could get anything for them. Although Jackie could not meet many of their demands, she was prepared to be used like this. Anything, in fact, to show the love of Christ. But, as a missionary, she seemed to be a failure. No one would believe in Jesus.

Then she had an experience that completely changed her life and work. One day someone showed her that she was trying to do God's work in her own way, not in His way. She was not giving Him the chance to help her, even though she truly believed in Him. When Jackie realised this, she prayed and asked God to give her a new power, to fill her with His Spirit.

For a while nothing different happened. Jackie went on with her work in the Walled City in the same way as before. But then she found that she could pray to God in a new kind of language. It was not English, or any other language she could recognise. It was a kind of heavenly language, for prayer and worship. In the Bible, it is called "speaking in tongues". Jackie prayed in this new language and found that God began to do wonderful things for her. Without much effort on her part, people believed when she spoke to them about Jesus, drug addicts came off drugs and she had remarkable answers to prayers.

The evening after the break-in at the club, Jackie noticed a young man leaning in the doorway of the club.

"Got any trouble?" he asked.

"No, everything's fine," replied Jackie. "Why? Who are you anyway?"

"Goko sent me," he answered.

Jackie was taken aback. She had often sent messages to Goko, trying to arrange a meeting, but he had never bothered to reply. He was the top Triad gang leader in the City, too important to be bothered with a youth club organiser – and a woman, at that. But now he had sent one of his followers to guard the club.

"Goko said that if anyone bothers the club again, we'll deal with them." He mimed thrusting a dagger into a victim's belly.

"Thank you very much," said Jackie. "Would you please tell Goko that I am grateful, but I don't need his help. Jesus is looking after us."

"You must be crazy," he told her.

This was the first time Jackie met Winson. Night after night he returned to take up his post as youth club guard. He watched the boys at their games, enjoyed the hymn-singing and listened to the gospel talk Jackie gave every evening. But he always stayed just outside, in the street.

Later she discovered that Winson had run away from home as a boy and joined Goko's 14K Triad gang. Winson's gang number was 426. This meant he had a special rank: fight-fixer. His job was to arrange fights between rival gangs and choose the weapons. He was a very tough gang member. Jackie also found out that Winson was addicted to opium.

From time to time Jackie spoke to Winson and explained that Jesus could help him give up opium. He refused to believe. One night, however, when most of the boys had gone home, she invited him into the club. He accepted, and started to join in the hymn-singing. Jackie realised that he had been listening to her all the time he had been guarding the club. He had made up his mind to believe, and was prepared to give Jesus a try.

When he prayed with Jackie, Winson straight away began to speak to God in a wonderful language. As he prayed, he was completely cured of his drug addiction. He gave up opium without any pain or trouble.

"Now you must go and tell your gang that you believe in Jesus," Jackie told him. "Don't forget, no man can serve two Big Brothers. You can't follow Jesus and Goko."

Winson went back to his gang and told them what had happened to him. He also told Goko that he believed in Jesus. This was a brave thing to do, as he might have been beaten up. As it was, Goko decided to let him go.

A meeting with Goko

Goko had discovered who had messed up the club-room. He told the boys to return anything they had stolen and to go back to the club and behave.

"Can't go back," one of them told him. "We've broken up the place. She won't have us."

"Yes, she will," replied Goko. "Miss Poon is a Christian and she'll forgive you no matter how many times you offend."

At least, thought Jackie, Goko was beginning to understand the message she brought.

Some time later, Goko finally agreed to meet Jackie. He invited her to a restaurant and ordered food and drink. For a while, they said very little. Like two boxers, they were sizing each other up.

"Let's stop pretending," Jackie said at last. "You and I have nothing in common, so why are you being kind to me?"

"I believe you care about my followers like I do," Goko answered.

The youth club Jackie started in the Walled City

"Yes, I do, but I hate everything you stand for and I hate what you do."

"Poon Siu Jeh, you and I both have power," he went on. "But you have a power I don't have. I can't make my brothers quit drugs. I've watched you, and I believe your Jesus can. So I've decided to give the addicts to you."

"No. You only want them off drugs so they can fight for you. If they follow you they will certainly go back to the habit."

"All right, then. I'll give up my right to those who want to follow Jesus."

Jackie was amazed at this offer. The Triads never gave up their members. Membership was for life: once someone decided to join, there was no going back.

"I'll tell you what," Goko suggested as a final offer. "You can have all the rotten ones."

Jackie smiled. "All right. Those are the ones Jesus came for anyway."

The pact was agreed. Since then Jackie has helped many Triad members to become believers and give up drugs.

Drug addiction

For many years Hong Kong has been a centre for illegal drugs. In 1980 a Government report stated that there were an estimated 40 000 drug addicts in Hong Kong, most of them men. This amounted to about one per cent of the population. It is thought, however, that the true figure was nearer 100 000. Most of these drug-takers were addicted to either opium or heroin, powerful drugs prescribed as pain-killers for people suffering from severe illnesses.

People who misuse such drugs quickly become "hooked" and have great difficulty in giving up the habit, just as people can easily become addicted to alcohol or tobacco. It takes only fifteen days of continuous use of a drug like heroin to become hooked. Drug-taking is an expensive habit, too. Few addicts can afford to keep buying the drugs they need, so most of them turn to crime to get the money.

If an addict decides to give up drugs, he must be prepared to suffer terribly. The "withdrawal symptons" last for three days. During this time, the addict breaks out in a fever, begins to sweat, has terrible stomach cramps and is violently sick. He may attack people around him. Even if he pulls through, the cure is unlikely to last. Many addicts return to drugs immediately after their "cure".

Drugs offer addicts an escape from the hunger and poverty of the real world, but staying addicted to drugs is like signing your own death-warrant. An addict doesn't look after himself: he doesn't eat regular meals, or wash. He may become depressed and try to kill himself. Death often comes early for drug addicts.

The Hong Kong Government is very concerned about drug addiction. Since 1981 it has been spending over £20 million a year in its fight to stamp out the illegal drug trade. To help drug addicts, the Government has set up twenty treatment centres and there are two hospitals run by the

Society for the Aid and Rehabilitation of Drug Addicts. In addition, many prisoners in Hong Kong receive compulsory treatment every day they are in jail. But, as one report puts it, "Treatment centres will be around for many years, until young people can be educated to avoid this dangerous attraction."

Learning by mistakes

One man who has been able to help addicts in Hong Kong is Pastor Chan, a Christian minister. He has a farm outside Kowloon where drug addicts can stay if they want to break their drug habit. After withdrawal they stay on the farm for eighteen months, until they are completely healed and have grown stronger. These men are the only ex-junkies Jackie knew who had not gone back to drugs.

When Jackie tried to help drug addicts in the Walled City

Addicts in a Hong Kong opium den

she made some mistakes. Meeting Ah Tsoi made her see where she had gone wrong.

Ah Tsoi was only fifteen, but he looked like a living skeleton. His huge eye-sockets were dark, his face a yellowish grey. He had been addicted to drugs since the age of ten, when his stepfather had thrown him out of the house. He needed at least £1 a day to feed his habit, and got the money by robbing people. He had already been to prison for drug offences and was now on probation.

At first Jackie could not tell Ah Tsoi about Jesus because his mind was never clear enough for him to think straight. She waited, knowing there would be a time when she could get through to him. Each day she gave him a little money. Although she knew he would spend it on drugs, at least he would not be forced to mug and steal.

At last Jackie got Ah Tsoi a place on Pastor Chan's farm. She bought him new clothes and took him there, but he stayed only a few hours. He ran away because he could not stand the withdrawal pains. Jackie never saw him again.

When she heard that he had run away, Jackie was heartbroken. She lay on the floor and wept all day long. She had done everything she could for this boy, and had failed. She was not angry with God, but she could not understand why He had allowed it to happen.

The next day, as she walked about the Walled City, she noticed again the hundreds of drug addicts, openly smoking heroin. She prayed: "It would be worth my whole life if You could use me to help just one of them."

When Jackie met Pastor Chan, she spoke to him about her problem. He told her, "Miss Pullinger, you will make a very good worker because you care." Jackie realised that in a way she had cared too much about Ah Tsoi. She now understood that if an addict was to be freed from the habit he must want it for himself. Jackie could not save him.

Then she remembered what happened to Winson when he came to believe in Jesus. As he prayed in his new language he came off drugs without any pain or withdrawal symptoms. This was the answer. Jackie realised that in some wonderful way God was able to release addicts from drugs without suffering.

A good man

Ah Kei was a Triad gang leader and controlled a number of areas throughout Kowloon. He had hundreds of followers. After several attempts, Jackie finally persuaded him to meet her. The meeting was arranged for just after midnight.

"Poon Siu Jeh, if you can convert me, I'll give you a thousand disciples," he challenged.

"I can't convert you, Ah Kei," replied Jackie. "You can only believe it for yourself."

He invited Jackie to go with him on a tour of the shantytown where he controlled the gambling and drug dens.

"Poon Siu Jeh, do you look down on drug addicts?" he asked.

"No, I don't, because they are the people Jesus came into the world to save."

"Are you willing to be friends with one?" he went on.

"Some people in the Walled City criticise me because I am more willing to be friends with an addict than with those who think they are all right," she explained.

This seemed to satisfy Ah Kei.

Soon he stopped outside a tin hut. He led the way inside, to a brightly lit room where lots of people were playing various gambling games. They were startled to see a westerner. Ah Kei held up his hand for silence.

"Don't be afraid, she doesn't look down on us. She's a Christian."

Ah Kei invited Jackie to preach to the gamblers. They listened politely to what she had to say, then Jackie gave Bibles to anyone who was prepared to read one. The same thing happened in several other gambling dens that night.

In one of the dens, they brought a man who was doubled up with pain to see Jackie.

"Poon Siu Jeh, are you a doctor? Can you take him to a hospital?" they asked.

"No, I'm not a doctor, but I'll tell you what I can do – I'll pray for him."

Some of the men sniggered at this suggestion. But they showed her to a quiet room and brought the man in.

"I'll only pray on one condition – that nobody laughs. I'm going to pray to the living God," Jackie said firmly.

They agreed, and everybody stopped talking. Jackie laid her hands on the man's head and prayed in the name of Jesus that God would heal him. Immediately, his stomach relaxed and he got up, looking surprised. He was completely healed.

One of the men asked, "Is this the living God you've been telling us about?"

When Jackie left Ah Kei that night she gave him a Bible. In the weeks that followed, Jackie visited Ah Kei and read parts of the Bible to him. One night he told her that God had been speaking to him. She found this hard to believe, but it was true. He had been reading his Bible and was beginning to understand what Jesus was saying. He sat down with Jackie and prayed, asking God to take his life and make him a new person.

For the first time in many months, Ah Kei went home to his wife. He gave up his control over the gangs as well as all the money he got from his illegal activities. But he did not give up drugs completely, as Winson had done, and the problem troubled him for some time.

As his drug habit continued, Ah Kei began to lose hope.

Jackie and Ah Kei (second row, centre) at a baptism party

He felt he could not be saved. At last he gave up and decided to go back to the gangs. He planned a couple of robberies to get some money, but they failed. Once more he turned to Jackie for help.

Ah Kei told her that now he really wanted to come off drugs. In a last effort, he threw away his drugs and waited for the withdrawal pains to come. When they came, Jackie encouraged him to pray like Winson had done. Although healing did not come straight away, he prayed until the battle was won. In three days he was completely cured.

With his old life behind him, Ah Kei began to tell his relatives about Jesus. When they saw the change in him, many of them came to believe.

Ah Kei's father-in-law was so pleased about what had happened that he gave a special party to celebrate. "Once I was a young man, now I am old," he said, "but never before have I seen a bad man become a good man."

The Society of Stephen

When Winson gave up drugs, he continued to live in an opium den – he had no other home. It was the favourite meeting-place of his 14K brothers. So, although he had started a new life, he still came under the influence of the Triads. He was often tempted to go back to the gangs.

One day Jackie realised what a problem young believers like Winson were facing. If they were to remain free of drugs, they must be removed from dangerous temptations. They needed a home, like Pastor Chan's farm, where they could get away from the gangs.

Jackie decided to begin by opening her own home to some of these youngsters. First she would have to find a larger flat. A woman in the City offered her a flat, at a cheap rent. The walls were crumbling and there was a hole in the roof. There was no electricity and no lavatory, but Jackie saw it as an answer to her prayers.

She and another girl repaired and decorated the flat, and even managed to persuade some of the boys to help. Soon they moved in with their first four boys.

For a while Jackie again made the mistake of trying to do too much for them. As well as continuing with her usual work in the Walled City, she helped to care for the boys in the house. She cooked, fed and clothed them; she got them jobs or places at school. It was hard work. To make matters worse, the boys had never been brought up to live normally. They were used to being up all night and sleeping during the day. They got up when they woke up, did not eat at regular times and went to work only if they felt like it.

As more addicts became believers, somewhere else had to be found for them to live. Two of Jackie's friends, Ric and Jean Willians, were already helping with the work. They, too, decided to open their home to the boys. Then, with gifts of money, two further homes were bought.

In the first House of Stephen

Now Jackie was able to give the addicts support for twenty-four hours a day. The boys needed plenty of love and security, and time to adjust to a new way of living. When they left her, she wanted them to go as responsible members of society.

The next step was to form the houses into a society, with a legally registered name. This would be important when dealing with the courts or if there was trouble with the rent laws. They chose the name "Society of Stephen", sometimes shortened to S.O.S. The name was taken from a passage in the Bible about a man called Stephen, who spent his time helping needy people.

During the first four months, seventy-four boys passed through the homes. No boy was taken in who would not agree to stay at least ten days. But to give themselves a better chance of breaking completely free of their old habits of drug-taking, stealing and fighting, they really needed two years' care.

Most of the boys managed to settle down in their new home. They learned to do the jobs around the house, to go shopping and to care for the new arrivals. They had lessons in reading and English; they also read the Bible together and prayed.

The change in the boys was so marked that outsiders began to notice it. Most days the boys played football on a pitch next door to a government-run drug centre. The Stephen boys looked so fit that some of the addicts came and asked what their secret was.

Money

Strangely enough, money was never a serious problem during these times. Ever since Jackie stopped teaching, money to support her and her growing "family" had either arrived through the post or been given to her by people who knew her. Friends also gave her things like food and clothing.

"What do you do for money?" Jackie was once asked.

She hesitated, not wanting to sound bigheaded. "Oh, God looks after us. We pray for money and God sends it."

"O.K., but where does it come from?" the man went on.

At that moment there was a knock at the door. An old man walked in and handed Jackie an envelope addressed to "Jackie Pullinger, Walled City", nothing more. In it was an American hundred-dollar bill from someone she had never heard of. She showed her visitor the note. He smiled. "Enough, point taken," he said.

Some of the boys helped raise money for the homes by polishing floors. They had been given a floor-polishing machine and decided to go into the cleaning business. Tony, dressed in white trousers and plimsolls, was the foreman. He was good at organising and was able to get jobs waxing and cleaning floors. In this way, the boys not only helped to earn money but also took the chance to tell others about the gospel.

Going to court

The phone rang in Jackie's flat. It was Mau Jai.

"Johnny's been arrested. Please get to the police station quickly," he pleaded.

"How do you know?" asked Jackie.

"Can't talk here. Tell you later." Then the phone went dead.

By the time Jackie reached the police station, Johnny had already been charged. He had also signed a confession, admitting to a crime. It was obvious that he was not guilty, but Johnny realised that the police were out to get him. As he had a record, they would catch him sooner or later. He was ready to admit to the crime, if only to keep on good terms with the police.

Jackie pleaded with him to tell the truth, but he would not. She even spent a whole month's allowance to hire a lawyer to help him. When he got up in court, however, something made him tell the truth. Instead of being a short trial, it went on for over a week. But, in the end, the police won the case.

When the verdict was announced, the strain was too much for Jackie and she burst into tears. The inspector in charge of the case asked why she was crying.

"Because he didn't do it. He isn't guilty," she told him.

"Well, he's got a record as long as your arm. I wouldn't waste your time on him."

"That's not the point – he hasn't done this one."

"This is Hong Kong justice," the inspector replied. "Even if he hasn't done this one, he's done others. It's fair in the long run."

"That's not right," argued Jackie. "The name of Jesus stands for truth. We are called to tell the truth in court."

By now, other detectives had gathered round to listen. They just laughed at her, then went off together to celebrate their victory.

Johnny was sent to prison, but was shortly released. He returned to drugs, was arrested and sent back to prison. Jackie often went to visit him and he was always grateful to her for the way she stood up for him in court. But it was two years before he finally admitted that he needed to accept the gospel. He became a believer and came off drugs. Later he got a job as a nurse – on a ward for drug addicts.

Leaving court one day Jackie heard a shout behind her. She turned to see a boy being led into the dock. He was waving wildly at her, trying to attract her attention.

"Poon Siu Jeh, I've been framed – help me," he cried.

Without knowing whether he was telling the truth, Jackie went to the magistrate.

"Your Honour, I am not familiar with the accused, but I think it possible that he does not have legal aid. Could you remand the case, so that enquiries could be made?"

Although this was unusual, the magistrate agreed. When she met the boy in his cell, she was given only two minutes to speak to him.

"Listen to me," said Jackie. "I have no time to tell you about Jesus. But if you call on His name, He will hear you. He is God."

When Jackie met him again the next day, the boy's face was clear and happy. He told her that his name was Sorchuen. He had prayed to Jesus for help and now felt quite different. However, he was found guilty and sent to prison. By now Jackie was sure he had not committed the crime. Once again she hired a lawyer and set about finding evidence to prove the case. A new trial was arranged.

The police inspector was annoyed because Jackie was taking all this trouble over what he said was "a no-good boy".

"Why waste time on a boy like this?" he asked.

"Because I believe he is innocent."

"But he has more than a dozen crimes to his name," he told Jackie.

"Yes, I know, but he did not commit this particular crime."

At the end of the trial, Sorchuen was found "not guilty" and set free. Sorchuen was just one of several people Jackie has been able to help in this way. But she always insists that they tell the truth.

Refugees

By 1979 the drug problem in the Walled City had become less serious and Jackie started to spend a great deal of her time working at a refugee camp, looking after some of the thousands of people who have fled to Hong Kong.

Since the end of the Second World War, millions of people in the Middle East and Asia have lost their homes or been driven from their country by wars, or because of arguments between governments or political parties. In 1949 the first wave of refugees arrived in Hong Kong from China after Communist forces took over the Chinese Government. When the Vietnam War ended in 1975, Vietnamese refugees also began flooding into Hong Kong. The population of Hong Kong shot up from 600 000 to over 5 million.

One of the biggest problems the Hong Kong Government faced was how to house all these people. Some of the refugees have been found homes in other countries, but many of them are still living there in large camps. They wait and hope that one day someone will offer them a home.

A group of orphaned Vietnamese refugees on an outing with Jackie and friends, 1980

The camp where Jackie worked is at Tuen Mun, a few kilometres outside Kowloon. It used to be a factory, but in 1982 housed 1700 Vietnamese refugees. They sleep 200 to 250 in a room, with just enough space for each person to spread a sleeping-mat on the floor.

One of Jackie's jobs was to assist a missionary doctor called Donald Dale, who opened a clinic at the camp. She also held daily classes for refugees who wanted to learn English, and ran a weekly meeting for Bible teaching.

Some of the refugees in the camp came to believe in Jesus. This started before they reached Hong Kong. As they escaped by boat, they ran into many kinds of problems. And as people often do when in trouble, they prayed to God – and had answers to their prayers.

When refugees on one boat ran out of food and water, they prayed. Soon a passing ship stopped and gave them new supplies. Another group prayed and a helicopter flew over and dropped them some food. When they reached Hong Kong, these people were only too ready to learn about the God who had saved them.

The camp chairman was one of those who became a believer. He had been arrested in Vietnam for trying to leave the country. In prison, he shared a cell with a Christian pastor, who explained the gospel to him. He expected to be put to death, but was instead set free. He finally escaped to Hong Kong. The boat he was in broke down and began to drift. He prayed to God; another boat sighted them and towed them to safety. It was this incident that made him believe.

In the early 1980s the drug problem in the Walled City began to get worse and Jackie has once again been spending a lot of time helping gang members and drug addicts. Many of the Triads have come to ask for her help.

In 1983, however, something remarkable happened: Goko, the leader of the 14K Triad, became a Christian. He was baptised and took the Christian name "New Paul".

Many of Jackie's former drug addicts have fully recovered and have begun to live useful lives again. One of the boys from the Society of Stephen probably spoke for all of them when he said, "I am happy for the first time in my life, and for the first time in my life I can smile."

BIOGRAPHICAL NOTES

Jackie Pullinger was born in Croydon, South London, in 1944. After leaving school, she went to the Royal College of Music to study the piano and the oboe. She gained her A.R.C.M. diploma and a degree in music. Whilst at college, she became a Christian and began to think about becoming a missionary. Her attention became focused on Hong Kong, but efforts to find a teaching post there failed. She finally took "a slow boat to China" and arrived in Hong Kong in November 1966.

The youth club in the Walled City was opened in July 1967, and the first House of Stephen was set up in 1972. Several more followed. Two television films about her work were shown in 1976 and 1978, and Jackie's book, *Chasing the Dragon*, was published in 1980. She has been invited to Holland, Germany, Singapore and Japan to preach in prisons and churches.

A HOME FOR ALL CHILDREN

The story of Dr Barnardo

Geoffrey Hanks

The school run by Tom Barnardo in the East End of London was very different from schools as we know them today. For one thing there were only three classes a week – one on Sundays and two on evenings during the week. The lessons were held in a donkey stable. There was just the one room, with a few rows of wooden benches and no desks. A stove in the corner provided the only heating in winter.

It was over a hundred years ago, in 1866, when Barnardo started his first school. In those days, if parents wanted their children to go to a proper school, they had to pay. Mostly only rich people could afford it. The result was that few people were able to read and write, which meant they could never get a good job.

The pupils at Barnardo's school went because they wanted to learn. Every class was full. Sometimes as many as two hundred children and young people crowded into the stable. The youngest pupil was about six years old, and the oldest was even older than the teacher!

The school was known as a "Ragged School". This was because the boys and girls who attended were dressed in rags – they were too poor to afford proper clothing. There were many such schools all over the country. The teachers had no training and were not paid for their work. They just wanted to help the children to learn to read and write. But Barnardo taught his pupils about the Bible as well.

The "Ragged School" – pupils outside the donkey-stable

Barnardo realised, however, that his pupils also needed work. So he took in extra helpers, who taught the boys a trade and the girls to make clothes for themselves. He was later able to find jobs for some of his boys.

When Barnardo first started teaching at his school he found it hard to control the pupils. They tested him with all sorts of tricks. Some of them threw rotten eggs and oranges at him. Once he was pelted with "pepper bombs". But before long Barnardo won the respect and admiration of his pupils. They began to realise that he really cared for them. They stopped their tricks and would allow no one to harm their teacher.

One night, going home after school, Barnardo discovered that six of the roughest boys in his school were following him. He wondered what trouble they were up to. Imagine his relief when he found out they only wanted to protect him! They had heard of a plan to attack him, and formed a bodyguard to make sure that he got back safely.

The young preacher

Tom Barnardo was a twenty-one-year-old student when he started his school in the donkey stable. He was training at the nearby London Hospital to be a doctor. Soon he hoped to go to China as a missionary. Meanwhile, on two evenings a week, he went around the East End preaching.

On one occasion he was leading a meeting on a street corner. A crowd had stopped to listen to him, including some who were obviously out for a bit of fun. After Barnardo had preached, he closed his eyes for a prayer. At that point, a mud pie hit him right in the face, stopping his mouth. The crowd burst into laughter, the guilty lad making a quick get-away.

But this kind of treatment did not put him off. As well as preaching, Barnardo also visited homes and public houses, selling Bibles.

At one pub he found himself in a bar filled with teen-age boys and girls. As soon as he entered, two big fellows jumped up and shut the door behind him. Barnardo sensed trouble and saw there was no way out of it. He decided to put on a brave act and walked to the centre of the room.

"I have come to offer you the Word of God," he told them.

"Chuck 'im out," somebody shouted.

"I will let you have the whole Bible for threepence," the student went on. "Or you can have the New Testament for a penny."

"Let's 'ave the books," yelled another boy.

"Be fair," said Barnardo, jumping on to a table. "These books cost me double the price."

Without letting him say any more, several of the teenagers, the worse for drink, leapt at him. In a moment the table was overturned and poor Barnardo was lying underneath it. He tried to escape, but was too dazed to do so.

When the lads had stopped fooling about, they let the student get up and sent him on his way. Barnardo managed to get back to his rooms only with great difficulty. He had two broken ribs, as well as being badly bruised. It was six weeks before he was better.

Later that evening a policeman called to see him. He urged him to take the gang to court. Barnardo refused. He had offered them the Gospel and did not want to end by having the law on them. In any case, he felt that he was partly to blame for going into the pub in the first place.

The boys who had attacked him were surprised when they heard he would not make a charge against them. They decided that, from then on, nobody would be allowed to harm the young preacher. Every day, until he was better, some of the gang called on Barnardo to see how he was getting on. Afterwards he was able to go about selling his Bibles without any more trouble.

Years later Barnardo said that this event did more than anything to open doors into homes in the East End.

Homeless boys

However, the most important event to occur, showing him where his future lay, came after school one winter's night.

School was over and the children had left. Barnardo was about to close the door and go home when he saw a boy warming himself by the stove.

"Come on, lad, time to go home," the teacher said.

"Please let me stop, sir," asked Jim Jarvis.

"Stop? Why, your mother will wonder what has happened to you."

"I ain't got no mother," replied Jim.

"Well, what about your father?"

"I ain't got no father either."

"Nonsense, lad. Where do you live?"

"Don't live nowhere," explained the boy.

"Well, where did you sleep last night?" went on the teacher.

"Down in Whitechapel, in a cart filled with 'ay."

Barnardo was startled by what he heard. Could it be true that this ten-year-old boy really had no parents? And that he slept out rough?

"Are there any other boys like you, without a home?" asked Barnardo.

"Oh yes, lots of 'em," was the reply.

Surely the boy must be telling a lie, thought Barnardo. But suppose he was telling the truth? He decided to put Jim's story to the test.

"If I give you a meal and a bed for the night, will you show me where these boys sleep?"

Jim Jarvis jumped at the chance. He had never slept in a proper bed before. And so half an hour after midnight, when they had finished their supper, the two of them set out.

They walked the streets of Stepney in search of sleeping children. At first there was no sign of anybody sleeping out on that cold winter's night. Barnardo was beginning to think that Jim must have made it all up. Then the boy led the way down a side passage, which ended in a high wall. Beyond was the roof of an old clothes shop.

"Where now?" asked the teacher, getting a bit angry.

"They're up there," explained Jim, pointing to the roof.

The boy climbed the wall and then pulled his teacher up behind him. And there, on the flat part of the roof, lay

Barnardo and Jim Jarvis searching for homeless children

eleven poorly dressed boys. They were all fast asleep. They were hunched up close to each other, to keep themselves warm. Their ages were from about eight to eighteen years.

"Shall I wake 'em up?" asked Jim.

But Barnardo had seen enough for one night. In his heart he prayed that God might in some way care for these homeless boys. Little did he realise that God would use him in answer to his prayer.

Next day Barnardo arranged for Jim Jarvis to be looked after by a family he knew. Later, when he was old enough, Jim was sent to Canada to start a new life as a farmer.

The East End

In Barnardo's time, most of London's poorest people lived in the East End. The number of people living in the capital was growing rapidly, and many of them were out of work. There was no unemployment benefit or social security in those days, which meant that people without jobs found it almost impossible to live. Those who did have a job received low wages.

Parents often relied upon their children to bring in some money. Children had to do odd jobs, like selling matches or flowers. Many of them were forced to go begging. If they returned home empty-handed, they were beaten. If the children earned no money at all, some parents turned them out and told them to look after themselves. Some parents even sold their children to cruel people who used them for cheap labour.

Housing conditions were terrible. There were rows upon rows of small back-to-back houses. Few of the houses had water or lighting. Some had a toilet in the backyard, but many had to use a bucket. Poor families usually lived in only one room.

To escape from their troubles, many grown-ups and even young people took to drinking. Nearly every street had its own public house. Pubs were open until midnight. It was a common sight to see people drunk at any time of the day. And when they had spent all their money on drink, there was nothing left for things like food and clothing.

Children were often uncared for by their parents. They were dressed in cast-off clothing, and went unwashed and hungry. When they were ill, there was no money for medicine

A homeless boy

or to pay for a doctor. (In those days there was no free health service. You had to pay for everything.)

Hundreds of children died before they reached their teens. Many were driven to commit suicide.

Thousands of children, however, found it better to take to the streets and look after themselves. If they could not earn or beg a few pennies, then they were forced to steal. At one time Barnardo reckoned that there were about 30 000 homeless boys and girls living on the streets of the East End. And on any one night there would be another 15 000 children who had no home but managed to find the money for a bed in a lodging-house.

Lord Shaftesbury

One evening, at a church meeting in North London, the speaker did not turn up. Without warning, Barnardo was called upon to take his place. He took the chance to talk about his school in Stepney. He also told of his meeting with Jim Jarvis and the homeless boys. By the time he had finished, many of his listeners were in tears.

Afterwards a young girl came up to him. She handed him a small packet. "I was going to give this money for missionaries," she explained. "Now I want you to have it for your homeless children."

Barnardo did not quite know what to do. He had never before been given any money for his children's work. But he could not refuse the gift. Perhaps, he thought, this was God's way of showing him what He wanted him to do?

A week later Barnardo received a letter from Lord Shaftesbury, who wanted to hear more about the homeless boys. Barnardo went to Lord Shaftesbury's home, where he met several other important people. After supper Shaftesbury asked about the children.

"Tell me, are these reports about homeless children true?"

"Yes, my lord," answered the student.

"I suppose you know where to find these children?" Shaftesbury went on. "Could you find any of them tonight?"

"Certainly," replied Barnardo. "Any time about midnight. I know of two or three places where they sleep."

So, just after twelve o'clock that night, a small group of men could be seen making their way through Billingsgate Market, near the River Thames. At first it seemed as though the visitors were going to be disappointed. There was no sign of sleeping children.

Then Barnardo noticed a possible hiding-place under a large canvas cover. He drew back the cover and pulled out a thin, poorly dressed lad. Within moments, other boys were found at the same spot.

In the end Barnardo had seventy-three boys lined up for Shaftesbury to see. A few minutes later the boys were being treated to a meal of coffee, hot sausages, and bread and butter at Dick Fisher's Coffee Shop.

Shaftesbury watched the boys gulp down the food. He turned to Barnardo and said, with tears in his eyes, "All London must know about this."

The meal was over by three o'clock in the morning. As Shaftesbury was about to return home, he shook the student by the hand. "God bless and lead you, young man," he said. "Keep up your good work."

Finding God's will

As yet, Barnardo had not thought of opening a home for the street-boys. His next move was to open a mission. This was to be a sort of club where he could hold preaching services and also have classes for children and grown-ups.

A group of Christians who had heard of his work gave

him enough money to buy two old cottages, opposite the donkey stable. He knocked down the inside walls to make a large hall. He called his club the East End Juvenile Mission.

On several days of the week Barnardo held services in the hall. As a result of his preaching many people became Christians. They joined together to start a church, with Barnardo as the minister. He stayed in charge of the People's Church, as it was called, for several years. Then, because

Dr Barnardo as a young man

the crowds became so big, he later bought a public house where he was able to have bigger meetings.

All the time he was doing this work he carried on with his training at the hospital. But he began to wonder if perhaps God was showing him that he should stay in London to care for the children.

He waited and prayed, wanting to be sure what to do. Then one day as he was reading his Bible and thinking about his future, it seemed as though God was speaking to him. He read these words: "The Lord says, I will teach you the way you should go . . . and advise you." This seemed like God's promise that He would show him what to do. All Barnardo wanted was some sign from God to be sure.

A week later it came. A letter arrived from a complete stranger, Samuel Smith, M.P. He had heard of Barnardo's work and wanted to help. If Barnardo agreed to stay on in London and continue his work among the children, Smith would give one thousand pounds. Barnardo kept the letter secret for ten days so he could think about the offer.

For a little while now he had been thinking of opening a home for some of his boys. He felt that all the good work done by his mission would come to nothing, if afterwards the boys had to go back to the streets. They needed a home where they could receive loving care and attention. With this money he could start a boys' home.

He wrote to Samuel Smith, accepting his offer. He gave up the idea of going to China and made plans to open a boys' home. The year was 1870.

Boys' Home

Barnardo rented a large house in Stepney: Number 18 Stepney Causeway. He set about making the place fit to live in. Walls were knocked down to make five bedrooms. Bathrooms, lavatories, a kitchen and a wash-house were added. Later, when the Home was enlarged, a chapel and a library were built on.

The floors were scrubbed, and the ceilings and walls whitewashed. Rooms were prepared for a "father" and a "mother" who were to care for the boys.

When everything was ready, Barnardo spent two nights searching for boys who were willing to enter his Home. He had no problems in finding enough boys, though there were always some who wanted to keep their freedom. He took in boys and not girls for a special reason. He was still only aged twenty-five and unmarried, and felt that he could deal with boys better than girls.

At first he chose only twenty-five boys, although the Home was able to take sixty. He did not have enough money left to take care of more, and he did not want to get into debt. This meant that for a while he had to turn some boys away.

One eleven-year-old boy nicknamed "Carrots" was very sad when there was no room left for him. He pleaded with Barnardo to take him in. He had lived on the streets since he was seven, he said. He had no father, and his mother had turned him out of the house. It was weeks since he had eaten a proper meal.

It was difficult for Barnardo to refuse, but he had made up his mind. He gave the boy some money with which to buy food, and told him that he could have the first place that became free.

But that was never to be. A few days later some market porters moved a barrel. They found two boys inside who appeared to be asleep. One of them jumped up and ran away, but the other did not move. He was dead, killed by cold and hunger. It was Carrots.

When Barnardo heard of the boy's death, he was stunned. He blamed himself for what had happened. He decided that no other child should suffer in this way, if he could help it.

He put up a large notice outside the Home. It said that no child without a home would ever be turned away. In future

The Home in Stepney Causeway

he would never turn away a homeless child, even if it meant getting into debt. From then on he kept every bed filled.

Young man with a lantern

Sometimes boys came to the Home and asked to be taken in. More often it was Barnardo who found the boys and invited them in.

He used to go around the East End three nights a week, searching for boys sleeping out. He carried a lantern so that he could look into the dark corners and other hiding-places where boys usually crawled for the night. He left at about midnight and got back at five or six in the morning.

Each time he moved to a different area. One night he would try the Thames barges. On another night he would go to Billingsgate Market or to Covent Garden. He visited fairs, factories and public houses.

His pockets were always filled with pennies and pieces of cake, to win the boys' friendship. For those who refused the offer of a house, he had cards with his name and address printed on them. Many boys who turned down his first offer, had second thoughts and came to ask for a bed.

Soon the name Barnardo became even more well known in the East End of London. People began to trust him and turn to him for help. Everybody thought well of "the Doctor", as they called him. (This was despite the fact that he still had not passed his exams at the hospital.)

One night a gang of boys attacked Barnardo as he was searching the slums for homeless boys. They knocked him down and stole his money, his watch and chain, and even his hat and overcoat.

An hour later they caught up with him again. They had realised who he was and wanted to return his things.

"If we 'ad known it was you, sir, we would never 'ave done it," they confessed. "Sorry about it, sir".

Twelve months after Barnardo opened his Boys' Home an important law was passed in Parliament. It said that in future all children between the ages of six and ten must go to school. School board officers were chosen. It was their job to see that children went to school, instead of working in a factory or walking the streets.

As a result, some boys were now more ready to accept Barnardo's offer of a home. It was better to go to his school than attend day school.

Boys learning a trade

Training the boys

Barnardo ran his Boys' Home in a very strict way. Every boy had to get up at six o'clock each morning, and be in bed by ten o'clock at night. They had to make their own beds, scrub the floors and wash their own clothes.

Every morning, except Sundays, the boys had school lessons. They spent every afternoon in the workshops learning a trade such as carpentry, shoemaking and printing. Some boys were apprenticed out to various tradesmen. When they left the Home, usually about the age of sixteen, they were able to get a job and earn their own living.

Barnardo also realised the need for healthy bodies. The boys had regular P.E. lessons, and there was a large yard where they could play football. Then, in their spare time, some of the boys had music lessons and were able to form a brass band. The band often played at Barnardo's meetings.

Each day at the Home began with prayers. Every week the boys had religious education lessons. On Sundays they all went to morning service. Being a Christian had made a big difference to Barnardo's life, so he wanted to share his faith with his children. As a result, many of these young lives were deeply touched by what they saw and heard.

Home for Girls

There were homeless girls as well as boys on the streets of London. So far, Barnardo had not felt able to help the girls, though he had often worried about them.

Three years after opening the Boys' Home Barnardo got married. Like her husband, Mrs Barnardo had also run a school for poor children, and she shared her husband's faith and ideals. Perhaps they could now take in homeless girls?

They already had a suitable building close to their home.

All that was needed was some furniture and household equipment. Mrs Barnardo took charge of the work and made all the arrangements.

At first only twelve girls were taken into the Home. They were difficult girls, and came from very unhappy homes. Nearly all of them had a record of crime. Over the next year the number of girls rose to sixty. Some of them were found jobs as cooks or as servants in large houses. All seemed to be going well with the new Home.

And yet Barnardo was not happy with the girls' progress. There did not seem to be the change in the girls' lives that he had hoped for.

Thinking about the problem one night, he had an idea. The girls should not be housed in one large building like the boys; they needed to be in a family, like ordinary girls. He decided that he would build a village of cottages, where the girls could live in small groups, looked after by a "mother". In that way, the girls would have more care and attention.

Some weeks later, as he travelled to Oxford by train, he talked to a friend about his plan. What did he think about it? The friend replied that they should pray and ask God what He wanted Barnardo to do. The two men knelt down in the train and prayed. Next morning their prayer was answered.

While Barnardo was getting ready for breakfast at the hotel there was a knock at the door of his room. He opened the door.

"Is your name Barnardo?" asked a stranger.

"Yes."

"I hear you are thinking of building a village for girls and that you want some cottages?" the man went on.

"Yes, that's true."

"Have you got any yet?"

"Well . . . no, not yet."

"Then I'll buy the first one for you," promised the man. At that he left.

It turned out that this man's daughter had died recently. He and his wife wanted to do something as a result of which her name would be remembered. The man had heard of Barnardo's plan and felt that this was just the thing.

When the news got out, other people soon began to offer to pay for a cottage. Before long there were enough offers to enable Barnardo to start building the village. Three years later the Village Home for Girls was opened at Barkingside, Ilford, in Essex. It consisted of twenty-five cottages.

With a family

As time went on, Barnardo found that there were more and more children in need of his help. Ten years after he opened his first Home, he had 1000 children in his care. By the time of his death the number had risen to 8000.

After a while, Barnardo was forced to enlarge the Home in Stepney Causeway. Later he opened a second Home in London, called Leopold House. Other Homes were opened in places like Birmingham, Cardiff, Leeds, Liverpool and Newcastle.

Any child was accepted, regardless of age, sex or religion. The greater the need, the greater the welcome.

Once again Barnardo began to realise that he ought to care for his children in a different kind of way. He saw that the boys would be better off living in a family group rather like the girls in his Village Home. Perhaps they could be placed in *real* families, where they would have brothers and sisters?

As the thought grew in his mind he decided to put it

into action. To find the right kind of families for his plan, he asked supporters of the Homes to help him. Instead of choosing the families himself, Barnardo asked his friends to suggest suitable homes to him. He especially wanted homes where the children would be made welcome and loved.

These new parents were known as "foster parents". They were not the children's real parents, but people who acted as mothers and fathers to the children until they were old enough to look after themselves. When the time came, the children could return to Barnardo's to train for a job before going out to earn a living.

The plan was a success. In the first year 330 boys between the ages of five and nine were boarded out in 120 families. Next he placed some of his girls, and then babies, with families. By the time of his death, twenty years later, he had placed over 4000 children in good homes.

Special care

Barnardo showed special interest in children who were either very ill or handicapped: blind, deaf, dumb or crippled children. Some were like this because they had been born handicapped, or suffered from some disease. Others had been badly beaten and injured by their parents, or had not been given enough food.

To begin with, he opened a small hospital across the road from the Stepney Home. Here he was able to visit the patients and even to be present when any of them had to have an operation.

On one occasion he was talking to a lady visitor when he had an urgent message. He turned to the lady.

"Excuse me," he said, "but I must leave you. I have just heard that one of my boys is dying. He wants me to sit with him and hold his hand."

As far as possible Barnardo placed his handicapped children with the healthy ones. In this way the healthy ones learned to care for the others.

But there were some children who needed very special care. For these he opened a Home for cripples at Ilford, called Children's Fold. A few years later further Homes were opened in Lancashire and Yorkshire for children with incurable diseases.

Now Barnardo was able to look after children of all ages and conditions. Yet his work was not yet finished and he still had two great plans to put into action. When it became difficult for him to find good jobs for some of his boys, he sent them to Canada, where they could begin a new life. And before he died he was able to see another of his dreams come true. He founded a training-ship, in which many of his boys were taught to be sailors.

Money

As the number of children in his care increased, more money was needed to pay for their keep. It cost £15 a year to keep a child. Then there were other expenses, like rents and building repairs. For several years his helpers received no wages but only their board and lodging.

How did all this money come in? As Barnardo put it, mostly "by prayer and appeal".

In the early days money came in because the older boys did jobs to earn their keep. Barnardo formed a "City Messenger's Brigade", for which some of the boys took messages for shops and business firms. He also had a "Wood Chopping Brigade" and a workshop where boys made boots and shoes to sell. By these means the boys raised nearly £2000 a year for the Homes.

When people saw the good work being done by Barnardo, they began to send money. Some gifts were small, others large. A lady came to Barnardo's office one day and laid three £1000 banknotes on the table.

"I bring you this," she said, "because your door is never closed to any poor child. God will surely help you."

The woman refused to give her name, and no one knows to this day who she was.

Whatever he did, Barnardo always prayed first. He found that God answered prayer, and his children never went without the things they needed.

One winter, for example, he realised that he needed extra blankets. He learned that the cost would be £100. He was sure that God would provide the money, so he placed the order. Two days later he received a letter and a cheque for that amount. The writer said that he felt the boys would need "more warm clothing during the cold weather".

During the course of his life Barnardo received over £3¼ million for the work of his Homes. Yet despite his efforts to avoid getting into debt, he died owing nearly £250 000. However, a fund set up in memory of Barnardo soon cleared the debt.

The man himself

Barnardo was a small man, smaller than some of the boys in his Homes. But he was always smartly dressed, and took great care over everything that he did.

He had a great love of children, and they found him easy to get on with. The children enjoyed it when he came to read stories to them. He often played with his children, and his pockets were filled with sweets when he visited them. He was especially tender towards handicapped children, and spent a lot of time making sure they were well looked after.

When the children grew up and left Barnardo's, he kept in touch with many of them. He asked them to write to him, to tell him how they were getting on. Every year, about the time of his birthday, he held a big party for them. He talked to each one of them, asked how they were and gave them his advice if they had a problem.

He was a hard worker, sometimes spending as much as sixteen hours a day at his office. In one month, for example, he received 27 390 letters and, with the help of his staff, replied to nearly all of them!

Although Barnardo had a large number of workers, he liked to pick most of them himself. He took an interest in all that they did. They were very loyal to him, even though he was not an easy man to work with. He could be stern and cross with his staff, but he was also kind and thoughtful. In turn they admired his courage and discipline, and the way in which he cared for them.

Although he suffered a number of illnesses, he kept on working as long as he could. In the end, however, the strain of running the Children's Homes began to tell on him.

When he died, someone said of him, "Earth is poorer, Heaven is richer."

BIOGRAPHICAL NOTES

Thomas John Barnardo was born in July 1845, in Dublin. Although regularly taken to church by his parents, at the age of sixteen he confessed to being agnostic. Soon after, however, he was converted to Christianity, and he spent his spare time teaching in a Ragged School and visiting the homes of poor people. In February 1866 he heard the missionary Hudson Taylor speak about his work in China. To Barnardo this was his call from God – he believed God wanted him to be a missionary too. In preparation for this work, he moved to London to train as a doctor. Some key dates are:

1866 Opened his Ragged School in the donkey stable.
1868 Founded the East End Juvenile Mission.
1870 Opened the Stepney Boys' Home.
1873 Married Syrie Elmslie. Opened a Home for Girls at Mossford Lodge.
1876 Qualified as a surgeon. Village Home for Girls opened.
1882 First Barnardo boys sailed for Canada.
1886 Boarding-out scheme started.
1903 The Watts' Naval Training School established.
1905 Died, aged sixty years.

There were also other Christians working in London at the same time as Barnardo, to help people who were poor or homeless. William Booth, founder of the Salvation Army, started his Christian Mission in 1865; Dr Stephenson opened a Children's Home in South London in 1869; Edward Rudolf founded the Church of England Children's Society in 1881; and Benjamin Waugh founded the N.S.P.C.C. in 1889.

BOOKS AND FILMS

MORE BOOKS TO READ

Free at Last
Martin Luther King, by Patricia Baker (Wayland)
Martin Luther King, by Kenneth Slack (S.C.M.)
My Life with Martin Luther King Jr, by Coretta Scott King (Hodder & Stoughton)
Roots, by Alex Haley (Picador, Pan Books)

Island of No Return
Damien the Leper, by John Farrow (Sheen & Ward)
An Inn Called Welcome, by A. Donald Miller (The Leprosy Mission), the story of Wellesley Bailey and the Leprosy Mission
Learn About Leprosy, by David Huggett (The Leprosy Mission)
The Story of Father Damien, by Teresa Lloyd (The Catholic Truth Society)

I Wish He Was Black
Apartheid, by John Addison (Batsford Educational)
Children of Soweto (South Africa Racial Amity Trust)
Cry the Beloved Country, by Alan Paton (Penguin)
Fighter for the Right, by Pat Barton (Lutterworth)
Naught for Your Comfort, by Trevor Huddleston (Collins/Fontana)
South Africa–The Imprisoned Society, by Allen Cook (International Defence and Aid Fund)
Trevor Huddleston, by Ian Birnie (S.C.M.)

City of Darkness
Alcohol and Tobacco and *Drug Takers,* by John L. Foster (Edward Arnold, Checkpoint series)
Chasing the Dragon, by Jackie Pullinger and Andrew Quicke (Hodder & Stoughton)
Drugs, by W.J. Hanson (Longman, Enquiries series)
Friend of Drug Addicts, by R.J. Owen (R.M.E.P.)
Prison to Praise, by Merlin Carrothers (Hodder & Stoughton)
Vietnamese in Britain, by Penny Mares (Health Education Council)

A Home for All Children

Ever Open Door, by Caroline Scott (Lutterworth)

Father of Nobody's Children, by Norman Wymer (Arrow Books). Available from Dr Barnardo's

The Story of the Children's Home, by Alan Jacka. Available from the National Children's Home

The Welfare State, by R. Cootes (Longman)

FILMS AND VIDEOS

Martin Luther King Jr (10 min), colour. A good brief film on the subject. Made by Britannia Films and available from the National Audio-Visual Aids Library, Paxton Place, Gipsy Road, London SE27 9SR.

Walk to Freedom (20 min), black and white. Concentrates on the course and consequences of the Montgomery bus boycott. Available from the Concord Films Council Ltd, 201 Felixstowe Road, Ipswich, Suffolk IP3 9BJ.

I Have a Dream (35 min), black and white. A more comprehensive film about the American Civil Rights movement. Available from Concord Films Council Ltd.

Day of Good Tidings (Leprosy Mission), *Lifted Hands* and *To Children with Love* (Friends of Vellore) and other titles are available from Concord Films Council Ltd.

The Life and Death of Steve Biko (30 min), colour. Available from Concord Films Council Ltd.

Tale of Two Cities (30 min), colour. Thames Television, available from Film Forum (dbw) Ltd, 56 Brewer Street, London W1R 3FA.

There Is No Crisis (29 min), colour. Available from the Anti-Apartheid Movement, 89 Charlotte Street, London W1P 2DQ.

Attacking the Dragon and *Hong Kong Style,* from the Hong Kong Government Office, 6 Grafton Street, London W1X 3LB.

The Cross and the Switchblade (115 min), colour. A film about David Wilkerson's work among drug addicts in New York. Unsuitable for children under fourteen. Also available on video. Available from National Film Crusade, P.O. Box 100, Westbury on Trym, Bristol BS9 4QH.

I Am a Refugee (34 min), *Only When It Rains* (11 min) and *Road to Survival* (40 min), all colour. From the U.N. High Commission for Refugees, 36 Westminster Palace Gardens, Artillery Row, London SW1 1RR, or from Concord Films Council Ltd.

Dr Barnardo's – The Changing Need (19 min), colour. This and other titles available from Dr Barnardo's, Tanner's Lane, Barkingside, Ilford, Essex IG6 1QG.

The Goal of the League (18 min), colour. Available from the National Society for the Prevention of Cruelty to Children, 1 Riding House Street, London W1P 8AA.

Kaleidoscope of Care (30 min), colour. Available from the National Children's Home, 85 Highbury Park, London N5 1UD.